HOPE YOU ENJOY
LIFE IN THE SUNSET

[Paperback]
ISBN 13: 978-1-58790-340-3
ISBN 10: 1-58790-340-7

[E-book]
ISBN 13: 978-1-58790-341-0
ISBN 10: 1-58790-341-5

Library of Congress Control Number: 2015954026

Manufactured in the United States of America
Regent Press
www.regentpress.net

Life in the Sunset is dedicated to the women in my life. Past and present.

LIFE IN THE SUNSET

Part 1

by Ron Jones

From the beginning this place was sand and fog. Home for creatures and plants ever changing. I was there for a moment. We all have this moment in that place we call home.

Regent Press
Berkeley, California

<u>46th AVENUE</u>

Down by the meadow
by the itty bitty pool
Swam three little fishes
And the Mommy fishy too
Swim said the Mommy fishy
Swim if you can
And they swam
And they swam
All over the dam
Boom boom dittum dattum
Why don't you?
And they swam and they swam
All over the dam

That's my mother singing. She's the reason we are here – this life in the Sunset, living on 46th Avenue in the Sunset district of San Francisco.

She wanted everyone to live in one big house but since that was impossible the next best thing was for the family to live on the same avenue.

It was the end of World War II and all these new houses were being built on the sand dunes of the Sunset.

We moved into 1492 46th Avenue on Kirkham. It was easy to remember our address – "Columbus sailed the ocean blue in 1492." The streets were alphabetical north to south – I J K L M N…Irving, Judah, Kirkham, Lawton and numerical avenues running east to west. We were on 46th Avenue a few blocks up from the Great Highway and the Pacific Ocean.

My mother's sister Maxine and Uncle Frank and cousins lived on 46th and Ortega. Maxine had been a dancer like my mother. Frank was a union organizer for the SF Postal Workers. The only communist in the family, at least for a while. He rode a Harley.

My grandparents Grace and Pop Calofsky lived next to the corner house on 46th and Rivera. My grandfather ran the President Follies in North Beach. They took in a homeless man recovering from the war. Pop found him sleeping in the doorway to the Follies under a blowup of Tempest Storm. His name was Willie. Somehow in the war he had lost his voice and spirit. He lived in the basement knotty pine room of my grandparent's house. When I was 12 this stranger, Willie, a man that never spoke, gave me the gift of 1000 voices. Most houses in the Sunset have a knotty pine room and a guest that is a stranger to all of us.

Taking in people seemed something my family did. My mother was always inviting friends and family members to stay with us. My father T.C. Jones always had musician friends needing a couch. It was something my younger brother Douglas and I got used to. One family stayed with us for a lifetime. My mother took in a friend of hers, Glenna and her two children Sandy and Jean. They were the same age as my brother and I. My mother and Glenna had danced together before children and the end of vaudeville. My mother couldn't tolerate her friend getting beat up and not having a safe place to stay.

T.C. Me and Mom

Glenna and Mom

Mom is third from right

SHOW BIZ

My mother grew up in the Mission. She attended Mission High but left before graduating to be a dancer. She was small and a tap dancer or hoofer. As a child she took the stage at Wigwam and New Mission Variety Shows – live entertainment and prizes to bring in an audience for the feature film. My mother and father opened the Fox Theater on Market Street – my mother dancing in the chorus line and T.C. playing trombone in the orchestra pit – that magically appeared accompanying 'Hell's a Poppin' comedians, ventriloquists, and dancers – live shows in an ornate palace and audiences waiting for familiar routines.

Market Street had a string of these theaters. Lots of work for show girls with long legs, hoofers or trombone players. Clubs to play. Gangsters to waltz around. Tours to nowhere. Hollywood calling. The unexpected when you're dancing on top of the world.

My mother refusing to remove a photo of the Nicholas Brothers from her dressing room mirror at Bimbos 365 Club. Ending a career as the naked lady in the fish bowl. Then there was that event in New York City. T.C. and my Mom in a touring show of big promises. The promoter refusing to pay the band and dancers until the show ended. It was a show that never ended until my Mom had an idea. T.C. always went along with her ideas. It was a simple plan. In the finale of the show as dancers trudged up a treadmill to heaven, singing, "Brother can you spare a dime . . ." – my father and the other musicians would tear up their music and throw their music stands onto the stage. Once on the stage the band would play faster and faster as my Mom hit the speed button on the treadmill! Singers were now flying up the treadmill into heaven and leaping into the arms of waiting musicians and stage crew. Then stripping off their costumes and dancing naked into waiting wings. Musicians are not good dancers. The show ended that night.

Problem was the NY critics. They loved the madcap ending. Proclaimed the show a Naked Hit!

The producer and replacement performers made a fortune. The San Francisco dancers and band hitchhiked back to the City.

While in New York my Mom turned down the job of choreographer for a new dance troupe at Radio City Music Hall that would become the Rockettes. She preferred returning to San Francisco and the challenge of directing the first all Chinese girl dancers at the Forbidden City. Being successful, she was fired by the women she taught and the man that hired her. All the while T.C. played Italian dirges in a band that weekly marched up Grant Avenue to honor the passing of a Chinese citizen. Usually men.

With the war, vaudeville became a fading memory. My mother worked for the government on Market Street managing the flow of personnel and materials for the war effort. Like the women of her time, they gained respect and positions of authority only to be dismissed for the men returning home. T.C. was one of those men. He was in the Merchant Marines. Actually he was in the Merchant Marine Band that played patriotic marches for men leaving from the piers at Ft. Mason.

It was no wonder the Sunset District seemed like the perfect place to
move. Lots of little stucco houses all in a row. A new place to start over. T.C. could get
gigs in the Golden Gate Park Band and at Sweets Ballroom in Oakland. Mom and
Glenna could start a dance studio in the knotty pine basement room on 46th Avenue.
And there was always my mother singing as if we were in some musical.

Picking up Grandma and all of us piling into the Packard for a Sunday drive. My brother
with his never leave home without a sandwich! Glenna, Sandy, and Jean. Weaving our
way down El Camino through the orchards and waves of yellow mustard. A perfumed air
leading us to Woodside, La Honda, then back along the coast. Sometimes all the way to
Santa Cruz if the Packard didn't overheat. And all the way singing, led by my mother.

Boom Boom
Ain't it great
To be crazy
Boom Boom
Ain't it great
To be crazy
Horsey and a flea
And three blind mice
Sittin' in a corner
Shootin' dice
Horsey slipped
And fell on the flea
Oops said the flea
There's a horsy on me

LOEWS
WARFIELD
Downtown FOX WEST COAST THEATRE
TODAY AT 11 a.m.!
LAFFS! LAFFS!
HE MISTOOK HIS ASTHMA FOR PASSION
A gay old dog, bitten by super love . . . dragged to the altar by a hot-cha mama . . . but the halter broke!
"BACHELOR'S AFFAIRS"
ADOLPHE MENJOU
MINNA GOMBELL—JOAN MARSH
ALAN DINEHART
A Fox Hilarity Hit!
Metrotone News
More Laughs!
ZASU PITTS
THELMA TODD
in
"THE OLD BULL"
A good steer for lovers of rare comedy!
ANOTHER STAGE THRILL!
Peggy O'Neill's WARFIELD
FOLLIES
Featuring the international star of stage and screen
ROSITA MORENO
With a stage full of glorious girls . . . snapping senoritas . . . riotous fun . . . tantalizing tunes . . . clever stars
ARMANDA CHIROT
Alice Hamilton . . . Bob & Eula . . .
Lester & Garson . . . Don Smith . . .
Geneva . . .
RUBE WOLF JOY-GANG

THE SUNSET

Whereas my mother being Jewish wanted to put curtains on the world and make it a safe and fair place for all – my father was simply content to listen to the melodies in his head and play his horn. He would drive to the beach to serenade a sunset. Everyday he polished his shoes and practiced his horn. Every meal he proclaimed as "this is the very best meal I've ever eaten!" My mother once confessed to me, "You know I married your father because he was the kindest man I'd ever met." Everyday in the Sunset was perfect, or was it?

The Sunset from my earliest memories was a place of wonder. On 46th Avenue there were still homes being constructed. They sprang from the sand dunes like wooden skeletons smelling of pine and providing great places to climb around and jump from. Driven by the wind, sand would pile up against the unfinished structures and be like waves you could jump into. Wooden street cars clanked up Judah Street to the tunnel leading to the heart of the city. These green and orange streetcars had cow catchers in the front and back that you could ride on. And wooden chairs with brass handles that could be flipped to accommodate the direction of the streetcar.

Great sand dunes still existed west of Sunset Blvd where Giannini Jr. High School and Saint Ignatius High School, now hold the sand in place. These dunes were home to mountainous sand and snake - like patterns carved by the wind. Sometimes you could be in these canyons of sand and all you could see was the sky. Usually shrouded in a summer fog – a white curtain that would wait for the day's end before lifting to expose the promise of light in a glorious sunset.

At the southern end of 46th Ave. there was Fleishhaker pool – the world's largest salt-water pool where Hawaiian lifeguards used rowboats and every morning, pan fried freshly caught abalone. Next to the pool the SF Zoo awaited visitors with the fabled monkey island and a whistling steam train. On the corner of 48th Ave. and Sloat a horse stable and paddock provided horseback riding on English saddles for proper trotting down the Great Highway and into Golden Gate Park. Around the corner from my grandmother's there was an ice skating rink and up on Noriega the Ali Babba Bowling Alley.

In the Sunset of my youth there were three lumberyards providing the building materials to fill in vacant sand lots with new homes for the sale price of fourteen thousand dollars. Judah, Noriega and Taraval were corridors of neon signs welcoming you to bars, restaurants, grocery, pharmacy, hardware and variety stores. Local plumbing, glass, and radio/ TV repair shops along with auto garages and gas stations provided services to keep everything running. Everything you needed was close by. Everything could be fixed. Shopping locally you received S and H Green Stamps for redemption and a discount on household purchases. Gas was 19 cents a gallon and included service along with a token plate or memorial glass. Big-ticket items like appliances or Easter clothing could be purchased downtown. You had to dress up to go downtown to shop at the Emporium or City of Paris. Women wore gloves and men wore large brimmed hats, suits and ties.

Drugstore 46th ave. and Judah

Gas station 45th ave. and Judah

Doctor Tucker did house calls and sewed up my bleeding dog bites on the dining room table. Then helped canvas the avenues to find the white terrier and determine if I needed a series of painful shots. A friend of my mother, Alvin Nadler, went door to door in the Sunset selling insurance policies and saving plans for one dollar a month. Mom cashed in these insurance plans to trade in the Packard and buy the first 'which way were you going in the Sunset' Studebaker automobile.

I suspect the future is evident in our everyday events. It's hiding but it's there. The people and things that surround you. Let me take you into my world of growing up as a child in the Sunset of the 1950's.

On the corner of 46th and Judah was Karl's Grocery Store. Karl kept a tab so I could run there to pick up a pack of Grandma's Chesterfields, a can of creamed corn, and jelly-rolls. Karl was our local banker where you could cash checks for free and get a loan if you needed to get by. Across the street from Karl's there was a pharmacy. And down the street on Judah a 5 and 10-cent store where you could buy 10 cent classic comics and Pee Chee's with life saving multiplication tables. Across the street and up from Karl's were two bakeries with an early morning smell of baked bread and cinnamon roles. All these stores were owned by people living in the neighborhood. The owners of the 5 and 10-cent store had a son attending West Point. Karl and the butcher Vince knew everyone on a 'good morning' basis and 'I'm here if you need anything.'

Karl was a hypnotist and my mother convinced him to hypnotize me to conquer my inadequacy in mathematics. I pretended this deep sleep worked and maybe it did. As for the butcher, he hired me to deliver and pick up packages. Not fish that everyone purchased on Fridays but envelopes filled with numbered sheets and sometimes bundles of cash.

We knew most of the people living on 46th Avenue. For the most part, the families were Catholic with children attending Holy Name. My mother hosted parties, particularly around the Christmas holidays, where all the shopkeepers and neighbors would crowd into our living room to share a Manhattan or Old Fashion and gossip about the changing times. And the yearly holiday event when T.C. would try to eat one of the ceramic elves thinking it was made of chocolate. Our home, like so many had a liquor cabinet displaying bottles of booze, a row of glasses and colorful toothpicks with olive helmets. My parents didn't smoke although everyone else seemed to enjoy a Camel cigarette or in the case of my grandfather, a Cuban cigar.

As kids in the neighborhood the street was ours. There was no television to bring us inside. So our parents let up play outside until it got dark. One foot off the gutter. Kick the can. Racing back and forth across the street that was free of cars and traffic. My favorite game was throwing a tennis ball against the stairs with everyone trying to catch a crazy bounce or line drive. Hating for it to get dark and our parents calling from the front door – "It's time to come in, I'm not calling again!"

Our house on 46th Avenue was a replica of the house next door and down the street. In fact row upon row of what would be called ticky tacky. Oh, there were the occasional

Our house 46th ave. and Kirkham

beach houses moved to the Sunset after the earthquake but these older homes huddled in the fog as if not to be compared with the newer homes built by Doelger. All the newer homes looked the same from the outside. A picket row of beige homes with fingers of grass reaching curbside. Some had tunnel entrances and internal patios but all had two bedrooms in the back, a hallway connecting the kitchen, bathroom and living/dining rooms. Off the kitchen was a breakfast nook and backstairs leading to the street and the tradesman entrance. Milkmen delivered milk and tradesmen still plied the Sunset selling fresh vegetables from their truck bed and icemen delivering huge blocks of ice. Men with black leather capes and calipers pinching blocks of ice for the icebox sitting on the back porch next to the kitchen. An event that would vanish overnight with the delivery of the first refrigerator.

Our house was my mother's greatest pride. The knotty pine room in the basement had built-in bunk beds hidden by a moveable mirror that became her and Glenna's dance studio during the day and bedroom for Glenna and her children at night. The walls of this room were covered with black and white photos of the vaudeville stars my mother and T.C. worked with. Elegant and stylish women and men in tuxedos starring down upon us like gods of a glittering era.

My brother and I shared the upstairs bedroom with wallpaper of Hopalong Cassidy and our own radio. Every night we listened to "I Love a Mystery" and later the jazz of Al Jazzbeau Collins in the Purple Grotto. Plastic and balsa wood models of airplanes hung suspended above our beds. P-38's and Flying Tigers to remind us of the glory of the war. Comic books were stashed beneath our beds to be read over and over. The Classic Comics of Treasure Island and the Man in the Iron Mask. Three Musketeers, Archie, and Superman to fill out our fantasies and tell us how to live. Tales of loyalty and courage. Good night prayers led by my mother or T.C. Then flashlights under the covers to read and become Prince Valiant.

Ron and Doug at home

THE FUN HOUSE

Elementary school was a three block walk up Judah to Francis Scott Key Annex. An immediate curiosity to a child. Why was I assigned to the Annex? It was a Frankenstein like building next to a block long pit surrounded by a chain link fence. Nothing like the modern Francis Scott Key Elementary School just one block away. It's interesting that I have a vivid memory of early childhood classmates but nothing to remind me of college days. Maybe its because I was with the same group of children from third grade to graduation into junior high school. And we had the same teacher, Mrs. Dawson.

With her white hair, shoulder padded dresses, and beak like nose, she looked like an American eagle. She introduced us to folk dancing, Standard School Broadcast, and each other. Under her tutelage we used pen and inkwells to scratch out a weekly 'this is a sample of my best handwriting'. She also conducted her every Friday 'We are going to die' Atomic Bomb drill. She would pull the curtains of the room and order us to "Take Cover!" Under our desks, on our hands and knees, we just looked at each other. Sometimes you could see girl's underwear. The room was bathed in sepia and sweaty as we waited for the blast of white light, which meant we weren't going home early. Our last vision would be Mrs. Dawson shoes and the American flag she held at her side.

Of course Bobby Ensign who lived on 45th Avenue would break the pending doom by asking Betty Jane Myers, "Could you move a little closer, over this way?" Bobby Ensign was a goofus. Big and clumsy for his age with a constant stream of ideas to save the western world. It was his idea to make up membership cards to the Communist Party and solicit membership in our secret club. It would drive Mrs. Dawson crazy if she found one, and she definitely would find one! After all, this was her fifth grade class and we were all going into her 6th grade or else.

We almost let Elaine Marsh join our secret party. Almost. She was rather tomboyish and could kick a ball to the fence at the pit. Not quite like Mike Hancock. Powerhouse! Powerhouse was the only one in our class that could kick a ball over the fence. Our only chance of beating the 6th grade at Francis Scott Key main building in kickball. But Elaine did have something we all cared about. In her basement on 43rd Avenue she had a ping-pong table. And her parents let her have friends over after it got dark. Bobby relented and decided to let everyone in Mrs. Dawson's fifth grade class join the Communist Party – if and only if – they passed the initiation test. This meant everyone was invited into his conspiracy. Even Stinky Weinstein and Winifred Lum.

The initiation was quite simple. Everything starts out very simple with Bobby Ensign. We would assemble in the Fun House at Playland on Ocean Beach. Sneak into the building when Laughing Sal was silent and the building was about to close. Then slide down the great wooden slide. Surely a great initiation for those wanting to join Bobby's Communist Party. Well, like everything Bobby proposed, it almost worked.

Just as the building was about to close, Bobby and I followed the worn footpath that allowed us to navigate the mirror maze entrance to the main floor of the Fun House. Once inside, we hid in the bathroom. We could hear the building clicking to close. We had done it. But where were Elaine and Betty Jane Myers? How come Powerhouse isn't here? And Stinky Weinstein. And Winifred Lum and everyone else. It was getting dark but we still had time to grab a burlap sack and climb the 138 stairs to the top of the slide. The air and burlap sacks smelt musty. Sitting on the sacks – down we went – the only two Communists in Mrs. Dawson's 5th grade class at Francis Scott Key Annex division!

That's when Bobby had an idea. Turn on all the lights and rides inside the Fun House. Of course he didn't ask my thoughts about this, no, no, he just climbed into the control booth that hovered over the main floor and started pushing every button in sight! Air busted from beneath the traveling bridge to lift up the skirts of girls, if there were any girls. The giant barrel began to tumble. The spinning disc below us picked up centrifugal speed to throw off would–be riders. "No, no Bobby, don't do that!" He didn't listen. Just smiled and pushed the Laughing Sal button. "OK, OK Bobby now this clown–like Laughing Sal is all lit up and roaring in laughter, just listen! Do you think Bobby this might draw attention to what we are doing, do you?"

We didn't wait long for an answer. There was a loud banging at the door. "Bobby I doubt it's Powerhouse trying to get in, OK, OK Bobby take a look – that's the police Bobby" – actually one Irish cop. "Well there now my boys what you be doin' here after closin' time, turnin' on the laughing lady, scarin' the neighbors?" Bobby tried to explain. "We are members of the Communist Party sir!" "Well now can you be doin' me a favor and turn off all this mischief?" Bobby clicked everything off. Sudden and awful silence. Just a flashlight shining in our faces.

"You look a little bit young to be communists, maybe I should be takin' you home so's you can explain this party of yours, to your parents and breakin' into the Fun House makin' a ruckus." Upon police delivery to my house on 46th Avenue my father just laughed. "Your Uncle Frank is going to love this – a communist in the family at last – Ronnie, it's a good thing your mother's not home. Let's just keep this a secret." "Good idea Dad!" Bobby's father, who was a San Francisco fireman, took the event a little more seriously.

He banned Bobby for 3 weeks from their basement and our radio project. This was serious! The radio project in Bobby's basement was our science project for Mrs. Dawson and it wasn't a volcano or electric potato but a radio to talk to the world. Remember I told you Willie Acker who lived in Grandma's knotty pine room gave me a special gift. It was a RCA Victor International Radio. You could turn the master dial and listen to international broadcasts. It came with two antennas. One that telescoped out the top and another imbedded in the cover.

Well, Bobby figured we could wire his basement to increase our listening and broadcast potential. Every basement in the Sunset was a shop of some kind - auto, wood, general fix-up with bottles filled with nuts and bolts. Tools waiting for use. Drawers filled with wire, clips and hangers, everything needed for a science project. Our radio project was our attempt to listen in on the world and broadcst our opinions like the DJs of the time. So Bobby's basement became a spider web of wires and microphones in a tangle of 5th grade great expectations. It was Bobby's plan to talk directly to the Russians. Tell them to stop scarin' us, that we were all brothers and sisters with common interests. "This is Radio Free Bobby a member of the Francis Scott Key Communist Party, can anybody hear us, come in, come in anybody!"

Grampa Pop on the right at his Burlesque House in North Beach.

THE ATOMIC BOMB AND THE INSECT LADY

This didn't ally our fears. I thought we should just build an Atomic Bomb Shelter. This time, Bobby went along for the promise of being Kings of the Leftovers. The both of us carried shovels to Grandma's house. My parents wouldn't let me dig a bomb shelter in our backyard but Grandma would let me do most anything. As long as she didn't know what I was actually doing. And anyway, I loved going to Grandma's house on 46th Avenue and Rivera. There were always these wrestlers that Pop promoted – Gorgeous George and the Sharp Brothers. Just hanging out around the kitchen table with ladies hired by Pop to work the President Follies – Tempest Storm with the flaming red hair. And the Fan Lady with red lips that slide off her face when she kissed you. Of course Willie would often come up stairs to sit and watch Grandma play her favorite conversation games over Chinese checkers and mahjong. And if I were lucky on my visits there would be Myron O'Malley. Myron, strange name for an Irishman selling brushes and household products door to door in the Sunset. Myron knew everyone. And Grandma liked his neighborhood gossip and products, particularly Wizard Wick – green bottle with a wick you could pull out to freshen your house. She loved the cleansing 'bubble gum' smell that blended with her burning of incense. There were these green Wizard Wick bottles with the fragrant stem in every room of Grandma's house. I guess it blotted out the aroma of Cuban cigars and made the house smell like – wizards.

Myron seemed surprised to see Bobby and I holding shovels. "Well there Ronnie me boy the problem with the Sunset is they're all just waitin' to die, don't you know, you be plannin' with dat shovel to be buryin' people, you not be hittin' anyone with that shovel now will ya? You know the problem here in the Sunset, they're all just waitin' to die!"

Myron was still talking as Bobby and I escaped down the stairs past Willie's room and into the basement. I had this treasure to show Bobby before we began the excavation of a Bomb Shelter in Grandma's backyard. It was in a box under the stairway. This is where Pop stashed his glossy photos of the ladies that paraded across his stage. "Look at these bosoms Bobby, better than anything in National Geographic!" Photos that Mrs. Dawson meticulously blanked out with swashes of black ink.

Further into the box there was another surprise – Pink Peeper Scopes. "Look Bobby, hold it in your finger like this and put it up to your eye. Now twist it – see the dancing naked lady, look she's naked!" "Wow, we could make a fortune selling these to 6th graders and it's got this nifty little chain, you can hook it onto your belt loop."

Digging deeper into the box there was a final treasure. "Oh, Bobby, look at this!" It was heavy to hold. Wrapped in a silken scarf that smelled of lavender. "Look, Bobby, a gun! A real gun!" It was a silver revolver with a pearl handle. My grandfather carried it to work but now it was in my hand. A gun with six bullets waiting to be pressed into the chamber. I always thought bullets would be pointed like a dagger and sharp but the nose of each bullet was round and almost soft. I loaded the gun and pretended to shoot Bobby Ensign. "Bang – Bang!" He rolled to the floor, grabbed his stomach and started laughing. Then planning as only Bobby could do. "We should put this in our bomb shelter, after the war there will be lots of things around, cars and stuff, we might need this!"

With two shovels we started digging just outside the backyard door under Willie's window. We could see the cement foundation. We dug under the foundation and into the layers of sand. We threw our efforts over the fence into Insect Lady's yard. Insect Lady had been a neighbor of Grandmas' for years. She was crazy. Always sat in her living room screaming at anyone that walked by her house. She never went outside into her backyard so the ever-increasing piles of sand would go unnoticed. Newspapers and mail were left unread at her gated entry. Myron was the only one to stuff the mail and newspapers behind the gate and bring her a weekly supply of Wheaties. I guess that's all she and her yappy dog ever ate. But Myron was about to leave and return to Ireland so he passed the Wheaties task to Bobby and I. "Well there now me boys, don't you be thinkin' she'll be needin' a kit, she'll not be eatin' a thing, if you don't stop by!" Perfect. It gave us a regular excuse to visit Grandma and continue digging. Every Saturday Bobby and I would take a box of Wheaties and place it in front of the gated entry.

Our shelter was progressing nicely. We were over 6 feet deep with room for two. We had shelves for water, peeper scopes and a special place for the RCA Victor International Radio. Grandma's house was beginning to tilt into our bomb shelter but that wasn't our biggest problem. The crazy lady next door stopped taking the cereal box we left at her door. This necessitated a visit by Grandma and I. Something I didn't want to do. What if the Insect Lady knew about the dirt in her yard and would tell?

Grandma and I stood at the gate to the house next door and pushed the buzzer. I held a box of Wheaties. Maybe she wouldn't answer. Maybe we should just leave the box and go home. My grandmother hushed my thoughts and once again pushed the buzzer. Then we heard a barking dog and metal click that told us the crazy lady upstairs had opened her entry gate. We walked into the cave like tunnel entrance and up the stairs to be greeted by a skinny yapping dog and partially opened front door. I hate dogs. A year earlier on my bike I had been chased down 46th Avenue by this terrier that took a bite out of my right testicle. I'm afraid of their barking and they know it.

Grandma pushed me past the scratching and jumping sentinel. "Ronald there is nothing to be afraid of!" I thought to myself, 'Just look around, there's lots to be afraid of.' The dog scurried down the hall. The hallway. 'Holy cow.' We had to walk single file. Grandma leading the way resplendent in her red turban hat. Garbage was piled against each side of the hallway. Newspapers, rotting food, remnants of clothing and dog shit created a canyon of filth. Insects scurried around and under each hesitant footstep. Every room we passed was packed to the ceiling with boxes and their overflowing content. Even the bathroom and toilet seemed clogged with putrid smelling debris. At the end of the passage I could see Insect Lady.

She was sitting at a red Formica table in a pink robe that hung off her frail body. In constant motion she was clawing at the bleeding sores that covered her face and arms. There was no other furniture in the kitchen just that one chair and screaming wom-an. "Insects! Insects! Insects!" With each scream she picked at her skin and tried to eat the scales trapped in her spider like fingers. Her scrawny dog circled us and took several nips at my feet before she scooped it up and in one spastic motion opened the oven door – threw the flaying dog into the oven – and slammed the door. The wretched woman before us pulled at her stringy white hair then gyrated with both hands tearing at invisible invaders. "Insects, insects, everywhere insects!"

Grandma tried to calm her by placing the box of Wheaties on the Formica table. Grand-ma touched her turban hat to make sure it was in place then spoke very slowly, "Irene, this is my grandson Ronald, we've brought you something –." Before she could finish Insect Lady's eyes widened, searched about frantically, then were gorged at by fingers that plucked at the openings. "Insects, Insects, can't you see them?" Her bone - like fingers now dug into the opening of the pink robe. Picking at the skin of her naked body. Eating herself alive.

Grandma turned and gently pushed me toward the hallway. As we slowly retreated down that decaying corridor, I looked back over my shoulder. The dog had stopped barking. Insect Lady was screeching and pulling her hair. And there on that red Formica table was a box of Wheaties – the breakfast of champions.

"Well, there now, the social service department they not be doin' a thing. The poor dear they be wantin' her to come down to their office to fill out some papers, she'll not be leavin' that house of hers, and the dog, it's been dead now, I'm sure of it – the problem here in the Sunset, sure as I'm telling you – they're all just waitin' to die!"

It seemed like a waiting game was taking place. Myron, Willie and Grandma made a kitchen promise. The lady next door would not be alone. They took turns sitting in front of Insect Lady's house. She wouldn't let anyone in. And she wouldn't come out. And she wouldn't be alone. They sat there around the clock.

"No one, I tells you, should ever be alone, not that poor dear up there, nobody."

Then one day, a Saturday, Bobby and I were about to finish our bomb shelter and the chair out in front of Insect Lady's house was gone. It was the next day, Sunday, that a policeman came knocking on Grandma's door. He was tall and the leather in his gun belt squeaked as he shifted weight. "Ma'am, do you know the lady next door?" Grandma nodded yes and reached for her red turban hat and overcoat. Took a second to adjust both then took my hand. The policeman spoke in a rehearsed way. "Ma'am hum, we're next door and not to alarm you but we had a report of a robbery and we have the victim. Do you know your neighbor, next door?"

My mind raced into self—preservation. 'What's a policeman doing working on Sunday? Maybe she's told them about the dirt and my bomb shelter, our plans'? I tugged to get away from my Grandma's grip but she just tugged back. "Yes officer, we know the lady next door, her name is Irene, known her for some twenty years." The officer seemed to relax as if he'd found a way to tie up his case. "It's hum, kinda strange next door, would you mind helping us try to figure out what's happened?"

My grandmother with me in tow followed the officer next door. The gate was open as we trooped up the stairs and into the house. Then into the hallway. My mind reeled in confusion, 'What happened here? Where's the garbage?' The hall, it has a strange but familiar smell of Wizard Wick. And the debris that piled against the walls – it's gone! All that remains is a stain on the hallway walls like the ring on a bathtub. Even the rooms that had spilled over with garbage were empty like hollow staring eyes.

As I approached the kitchen I could see the red Formica table. My grandmother now pushed me backward so that I would not be able to enter the kitchen. Or see what the policeman was talking about. There must have been another officer in the kitchen, I could hear his voice but couldn't see him. "Ed, what do you think of this?" The first policeman that had come to Grandma's house answered as if in a rush. "I have the neighbor here, hum, I'm sorry – ." He turned to my grandmother who answered his questioning hands. "Grace, and this is my grandson Ronald."

I squirmed trying to look into the kitchen and the subject of the officer's attention. My grandmother simply shifted her coat and blocked my view. She would be very good in dodge ball. My attention turned to the hallway and the corners of the kitchen not blocked by Grandma's hand or overcoat. 'Holy cow, can't they see? Can't they smell? Myron's Wizard Wick bottles everywhere. That pungent sweet smell.'

The officer in the kitchen broke my fixation with his own. "Ed, take a look at this, she's all dressed up, make up and everything like she's going someplace." That did it. I cranked my head around Grandma's hand to see the body of Insect Lady sitting at the table. Like she was getting ready to go to church or shopping. She was wearing lipstick and her clothes, oh God, don't they know – that's my Grandma's best dress and shoes.

"Shot just once Ed, she's dead as a door nail." Grandma tightened her grip around my hand to silence my thoughts. "Yea, must have been a robbery gone wrong, look, they cleaned out the place – everything gone, furniture, appliances, and nothing left, just this red table." The officer I couldn't see asked, "So do you know her?" My grandmother answered, "Yes." "And how's about this fellow Myron, the folks in the neighborhood tell us he knew her and just about everything that goes on in the Sunset?" Speaking very calmly my grandmother stared straight ahead. "He's gone now."

The officer that creaked every time he moved seemed ready to get back to the Taraval Station. "Yea, it's just another killing in the Sunset – for what – some furniture?"

I was visibly shaking as Grandma and I spilled into the wet and salty air outside Insect Lady's house. Willie was there waiting for us. He quietly took Grandma's arm.

My mind recoiled, 'Can't they see, can't they smell?' Grandma knew my concerns as I burst into tears. "She deserved to die Grandma, she was crazy Grandma, crazy, crazy she killed her dog Grandma and she was, she was – ." Grandma held me very tightly so I wouldn't run away. Then she wiped away my tears with a silken scarf that smelled of lavender. The smell. The scarf. It had held the gun in the basement. "Oh God, Grandma, Grandma." She sensed my sudden awareness and confusion.

She pointed into the gray sky of the Sunset and the seagulls circling overhead. "Ronald, her name was Irene. She could tell weather by the flight of seagulls. She had these minia-ture red roses in her front yard, that every morning, Pop would put one in his lapel, every day, before going to work. And did you know she loved to dance, even went to Sweets where your Dad plays. She was a wonderful and kind woman with friends and neighbors that loved her."

I broke away from my Grandmother's arms and raced into her house and into the base-ment. The gun that I had found in the box under the stairs was gone. The Atomic Bomb Shelter in Grandma's yard was filled in.

I used to think danger was an irrational act and would come from far away. Danger is as close as a box in your grandparent's garage. And as for murder – murder is rational.

Close the windows, they're coming through the windows
Close the doors, they're coming through the doors
Close the chimney, they're coming down the chimneys
Whoops, look out they're coming through the floor
Boom Boom, ain't it great to be crazy
Boom Boom, ain't it great to be crazy . . .
Horsey and a flea and the three blind mice
Sitting in a corner shooting dice
Horsey slipped and fell on the flea
Whoops said the flea there's a horsey on me

S! — Give Your of
ROAR
GEE! WHAT A RACKET!
IT SOUNDS LIKE AN AIRPLANE
WOW! WHAT A NOISE!

<u>MR. GILLMAN</u>

Growing up as a child in the Sunset I was always surprised by the unexpected. Evidence of human behavior that would change my life. Lessons that I would learn about others and myself. The person that I might become. Like meeting Mr. Gillman.

In San Francisco in the 50's children were safe to play on the streets into the night or travel alone or with friends across the city. On my own, I went to Chinatown to buy fireworks or North Beach to visit grandpa and pick up a pocket full of peeper scopes. I could ride my bike to the Museum of Natural History across from the band shell in Golden Gate Park and just leave it propped up on its kickstand. It would be there when I finished looking at the medieval armaments and World War 1 tank. On weekends I'd take the N Judah downtown to trumpet lessons at Sherman and Clay. Or go on my own to the Emporium on Market during Christmas to enjoy the rides on the roof.

One of my favorite walks was down 46th Ave. to the Surf Theater or into Golden Gate Park. On regular treks down 46th Ave. I'd always stop at Mr. Gillman's. He lived in one of the original beach houses that preceded the mass produced Doelger homes. I was attracted to him immediately. He wore airman goggles and in the garage of his 46th Ave. home he was building an airplane. Not the balsa wood and plastic model planes my brother and I assembled, but a real airplane!

On my daily walks down 46th into adulthood I'd always stop at Mr. Gillman's to see and hear about his progress. All the parts carefully falling into place like a jigsaw puzzle. The under carriage. Control wires to the tail section. Instrument panel in the seat cockpit. The smile on his face. The concern of mine when the great wings were affixed onto the fuselage. He had built an airplane in his garage but had no way of getting it out! That didn't stop my regular visits. Mr. Gillman was always busy turning the propeller or painting lightning strikes on the body of the Piper. He had maps and weather reports to share. And always that knowing look.

When his house burned down and he was killed in the fire, people joked that he was nuts and eccentric. But I knew him as the builder of an airplane. I suspect many of us have dreams in our garage or scribbled away in a never to be read journal. But that doesn't stop us from dreaming. Putting on a funny hat. Building an airplane stuck in place. When I hear people say, "Why in the world are you doing that?" a familiar smile takes hold of my spirit. And I quietly smile. A secret smile that Mr. Gillman would understand.

FREE ENTERPRISE

If Mr. Gillman was a prediction of what I'd be, so was my attempt at free enterprise in Golden Gate Park. At the lower end of the park adjacent to the anti - aircraft battery, what is now the soccer field, there was a nine - hole golf course. I felt safe and intrigued by the temporary tented soldiers, their artillery guns and eventual white tipped NIKE missiles that pointed skyward. And older men comfortably playing golf under the fluttering American flag. Old men losing their golf balls into the rough. It was a business opportunity just handed to me. In fact, it bounced in front of me – an errant shot. At my feet. So round and white with dimples and scrub marks. I could see the man that hit the ball angrily swinging his club like a weed cutter. I grabbed the ball and walked up to him on the sloping fairway. He studied the ball. I had no idea a ball might have a special identity. Then he smiled and gave me a dollar.

A dollar was a fortune in those days. It cost 10 cents to get into Sutro Baths, Fleishhacker Pool or the Fun House. A matinee ticket at the Surf Theater was 20 cents. The number of golf balls in search of owners multiplied in my head. A business was born. I convinced Bobby to join me in the Ron Jones I found a golf ball enterprise! I chose Bobby because he was big and might be helpful if I needed muscle to protect my business. Although the truth is, Bobby hated to fight. It's interesting big men don't like to fight, it's the scrawny guys you have to look out for.

Our business started out with us just hunting the rough areas around the greens and then expanded to the perimeters of the course. We found a few balls but it was a lot of work. Then it struck us – why not run onto the fairway, often out of sight of the golfer that hit the shot and just grab the ball. Within an hour we had stolen over 20 balls. It was my job to take them home and scrub them clean so that we could return to the golf course the following week to sell them to golfers always looking for a cheap and clean ball to add to their bag. We sold balls for 25 cents each. It was all going well until I sold a ball to a golfer that seemed to know us. "You're those little communist pricks aren't you?" Before I could retort about Robin Hood, his partner bellowed, "The short one's in safety patrol at Francis Scott Key!" Selling stolen property to two policemen, just my luck. There is an adage in San Francisco that everyone knows everyone. It sure is true. Before he could reach out and corral me, I was off and running. Bobby was close behind.

<u>RUNNING WILD</u>

Running. Now that's the one thing I could do. I was the shortest kid in my class at Francis Scott Key but I was also the fastest runner. Everyone needs something that sets you a part. Makes you feel accepted. For Powerhouse, it was kicking a ball. Elaine Marsh had ping-pong. And Winifred Lum, she was just beautiful. If you had something special you were safe from ridicule or in my case avoiding arrest. You had an identity that you could hold on to like a life raft.

Everyday coming home for lunch I'd race down the avenue hurdling the patches of grass that stretched curbside. At a YMCA sponsored track meet in Redwood City, I had taken first place in the 50 and 100 - yard dash. Then used my speed to win the broad jump and high jump. It was known in the neighborhood that I was the fastest kid around. I thought I was the fastest human in the world until one day my mother challenged me to a race. "Honey, to the telephone poll and back." I wanted to show her just how fast I was so I started a second before she said go! She breezed past me like I was standing still. Just stood there waiting for me to finish. Then grabbed me and held me in a tight hug before whispering in my ear, "Ronnie, there will always be someone faster!"

Of course I didn't believe her, just worked to get faster by running in the sand dunes at Ocean Beach. Entered track meets for boys my size and age. Determined to win. In a city track meet at Kezar I heard the gun in the tunnel and ran as fast as I could. I closed my eyes and pumped my arms as if there was no tomorrow. Then suddenly I felt as if someone had knocked me over. I was on the cinder track and bleeding. I could hear the crowd yelling for me. I must have won. They were cheering for me. No, no, they were laughing at me. I had raced across three lanes with my eyes closed and smashed into the stadium wall a good 20 feet from the finish line. Bobby Ensign was there. He under-stood how I felt. The embarrassment, the feeling of being a loser. Being alone. Laughed at! He did something I'll never forget. He walked up to me and cradled me in his arms. Then reached into his jacket and gave me his first place ribbon. It was a gift of friendship that I still posses in a top desk drawer. And a lesson I would learn over and over. 'There's more ways to win than coming in first.' It's a hard lesson.

<u>SNOW WHITE VS GOD</u>

I hated being a loser but it seemed our fate with Mrs. Dawson's class. The main building always beat us in kickball, spelling bees, and May pole celebrations. And in the Safety Patrol Annual Parade at the Polo Field in Golden Gate Park, we always came in behind the parochial schools. You see, they had built—in uniforms that made them look organized and snappy. Those dark blue and maroon sweaters that made the white webbing of the safety patrol belt pop out. All we had was dark pants and white shirts. And our shoes never matched like the black loafers worn by Holy Name, St. Cecilia's, and a long list of sainted schools. Let's face it, they had God on their side. All we had was Elaine Marsh. She wanted to be in our safety patrol. But she was a girl. Can't have girls in the safety patrol. That is, until she showed us how we could win the Annual Safety Patrol Pageant. The mayor would be there. And members of the high school ROTC that trained us to march. Family members and a mounted police unit. It was a big deal.

The best marching team would win a banner for their school. The mayor himself would affix it to the flag standard carried by the lead marcher for each school. Being the smallest marcher, that would be me. Every school in the city took part. In previous years we had placed 33rd – one place above a school that failed to attend. I often placed the blame on Bobby. He had two left feet and often skipped when he got excited. The shoe stores in the Sunset all had an x-ray machine, which allowed Bobby to show me he actually had a left and right foot with radiated skeleton toes.

Elaine had a shoe plan of her own for marching to win. Her secret was a 'bunny bag' of white chalk dust girls used to clean their buck shoes. She argued, "If we all had white shoes, we'd stand out!" It makes perfect sense except for one thing. Most of the boys in patrol wore desert boots, brown wing tips, or keds. That's when Bobby chimed in, "We spray paint our shoes white then buff them just before the parade so they look all the same." Elaine smiled, "Snowy White! They have God on their side, we have Snow White."

The plan had only one unforeseen consequence. Marching in front of the mayor to Irish bagpipes with dignitaries from near and far – our shoes gave off puffs of white. With each step we set off tiny white clouds. Puff, puff, puff, puff, all the way down the course. Catholic kids holding their mouths to stop from bursting out in laughter. Then snickering and pointing at us. We had to just stand at attention as the mayor walked past us and made a joke about our shoes. The American sense of superiority of deciding who's in and who's out was beginning to take a strangle hold over my being. I wanted to be in. To be a winner. Elaine was crying and I didn't know what to do. Or more precisely didn't have the courage to confront something all wrong. A girl crying underneath the American flag. No, I was a coward. Comfortable to stand with our flag and say nothing to a person that risked everything to be a part of the safety patrol.

I was just like the celluloid heroes I saw every Saturday matinee at the Surf. The Road Runner being chased by the coyote. Don Winslow of the Coast Guard battling German spies. Americans killing Japanese in the Sands of Iwo Jima. John Wayne shooting Indians or anyone that didn't wear a white hat. Cruelty and a sense of superiority just underneath our celluloid skin. To be a winner or a looser. To be better than those around you. To survive. The choice came sooner than expected.

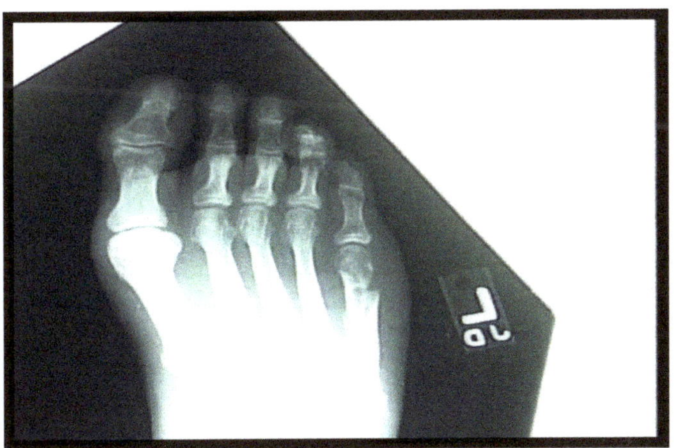

<u>STINKY</u>

It was Easter. All of Mrs. Dawson's 6th grade class brought eggs to boil and color. We made baskets out of colored construction paper. Flimsy but capable of holding the required half dozen eggs. I don't know how it got started. Or who yelled out – "Stinky Stinky Stinky Weinstink!" Donald Weinstein had been in our class since the second grade. He didn't participate in dodge ball or kick ball and often sat quietly on the bench during recess. He wasn't a milk monitor or a part of safety patrol. Didn't help put up the school's American flag or lead in the pledge. In fact, didn't say much. Just looked at you with scared eyes. Like he was waiting for something awful to happen. It sweated out of him like some oily fate. Made his eyes sweep the floor or dart away from your stare. His hands shaking as he held those Easter eggs. Then I heard the yelling a second time. This time it was louder. It came from the girls clustered around the girl's bathroom. "Stinky, Stinky, Stinky -." Winifred Lum was the only one not taking part in the taunting. She clung the basket of eggs next to her heart and looked away. "Stinky, Stinky." That's when he broke from sitting on the bench and started running.

The eggs spilled from his basket as he ran in a frenzied half circle. Eyes wide searching frantically for a gate to escape through. Led by Elaine Marsh, the girls sensed a wounded animal and started to chase him. Bobby, Powerhouse and I hesitated and then like everyone started running toward Donald. Trying to corner him. Trap him. Eggs were spilling onto the playground asphalt and being pulled from baskets. Someone threw an egg that splattered against Donald's back. Another egg hit him square in the face. Surrounded by us, he circled, turning first one way and then back. I picked up the only egg left in my basket, held it over my head and yelled, "Stinky Stinky Stinky – ." He spun and headed for the chain link fence that surrounded the open pit. There was no escape. He climbed onto the fence and just hung there like Jesus Christ on a playground cross. I ran forward, took aim, and let him have it! It felt good like I had killed a dying animal suspended before me. Donald mumbled for us to stop. To just stop. But we couldn't. Everyone was yelling and throwing eggs at this helpless figure. Then as if on some heinous cue we turned and simply walked away. I could hear Donald sobbing, asking "Why?"

He had never done anything to hurt me. I really didn't know him and never took the time to find out what he liked or what he did. I knew it felt temporarily good to feel better than that soul hanging on a fence. He did smell. And he was different. And I think he was Jewish although that was never spoken out loud. And for that matter my mother is Jewish so that makes me Jewish. My mind tumbled into confusion. Then regret. I knew I had done something terribly wrong. And I'd never be able to take back that moment with an egg in my feverish hand. Wanting to hurt someone that was different. Wanting to feel in control and powerful by abusing someone. To be a part of the 'in group'. To know superiority over those that were not like me.

Oh, I tried to find excuses. To make compensation. I gave Donald Weinstein my stamp collection and a bag of foreign coins from Pop's theater. One afternoon Donald asked me to come home with him after school to meet his mother. She greeted me with a firm handshake and a mother's delight. "Hello, I'm so glad Donald finally has a school friend." Some friend. Little did I know I'd be in his shoes sooner than I thought.

<u>HELL</u>

With graduation from Mrs. Dawson's 6th grade, we were propelled into hell! Junior High School. Since a junior high school didn't exist in the Sunset, we were to be bused to Presidio Jr. High across the park in the Richmond District of San Francisco. Of course the early morning pick up and afternoon drop off was the Francis Scott Key main building under the flag. The eighth and ninth graders had already taken their seats in the back of the yellow bus. Just sitting. Waiting for us. We were dressed in our best school clothes. The girls in gingham dresses and a few of them wearing sweaters that told of things to come. They crowded all on one side of the bus aisle behind the driver. They kept giggling and looking at the older boys in the back of the bus. Why is it girls always prefer older men? It's the way they look over their shoulder that drive men crazy.

Bobby and I along with Powerhouse, Stinky and all the other 7th grade boys took seats across from the girls. I was wearing my favorite pegged slacks with the cuff turned up a perfect one inch. A long sleeve white shirt and a cardigan sweater. A new leather belt and orange glow socks peeking out from the top of my Buster Brown loafers. My mother had packed me a lunch in a paper bag of a peanut butter and jelly sandwich, a plastic cup of Del Monte mixed fruit and a jellyroll. My father gave me 50 cents in case I needed to buy something.

I called "shotgun" and slipped into a seat next to a window away from those noisy girls. Bobby squeezed in next to me. By stepping onto that bus we had gone from being 'Kings of the World' to the 'Wretched of the Earth'. Our trip started out quietly. The bus huffed its way down Lincoln Way to the Great Highway. Then we heard it. A strange haunting song being sung by the boys in the back of the bus. "Dirty Lil, dirty Lil, lives on top of garbage hill, never washes, never will - ." I turned to Bobby as that refrain repeated over and over. "Hey Bobby this is great, they are singing to us, there's going to be girls at Presidio, this is junior high, they'll be wearing bras!"

That's when the singing took on an ugly turn. "Dirty Lil, dirty Lil, lives on top of garbage hill, never washes, never will - huh thu!" "Bobby, Bobby, they're spitting on us. Spitting, spitting, they're spitting, jeez!" And that's the good thing they did.

The older boys from the back of the bus now charged down the aisle spitting and grabbing at us – screaming, "Pants, pants we want pants!" In one violent tug I was wrenched from my window seat. Bobby tried to hold onto me but his arms were batted away. He was punched in the mouth and bleeding.

The girls on their side of the aisle sat petrified and staring in curiosity as I was dragged to the back of the bus to the chant of "Pants, pants, we want pants!" Both my arms were pulled behind my back. I kicked at my tormentors and tried to grab any seat handle but felt myself being pulled closer and closer to the back row of seats and jeering 8th graders. I was pushed onto the back row as hands from every direction picked and pulled at my clothing. I felt my loafer being pulled off and to my horror being thrown out an opened window. 'My God, they've thrown my shoe out the bus window, my mother's going to kill me!' My plea of "You can't do that!" brought a surge of laughter and a chant of "Pants, pants, we want pants!"

I yanked one hand free and tried to hold onto my belt but it was useless. I felt the belt sliding around my waist and then held in the air like some trophy. "Belt, belt, we have belt!"

I was surrounded now by hands holding me down, pulling down my pant's zipper, then my pants at my waist and now around my ankles. In the jostling chaos I could see down the aisle. Heads bobbing, smiling, looking to see what was happening. I kicked as hard as I could but that only made things worst. My pants were suddenly free and being swung like a cowboy lariat to the cheers of "Pants, pants we have pants!"

I closed my eyes to avoid the sight and hoped if I just went limp they would stop. That would be enough. Their game would be over. The bus was speeding down the Great Highway and soon would be heading up Geary to Presidio. To a loud cheer I looked up to see my pants being thrown from the bus.

I didn't know what I'd do but I thought the worst was over. I'd have to trace back the route of the bus and get my shoe and pants, but I would do it. I could run fast and make it back home. The arms holding me down suddenly relaxed only to be rekindled by a solitary voice that quickly grew into a catcall. "Under under underwear let us see your underwear – Tally tally tallywacker let us see your tallywacker!"

Oh no, I grabbed at the waistband of my new jockey shorts. "No, no, you can't do that, please don't do that, please!" Several boys forced me to stand on the back seat as my underwear was pulled past kicking legs and thrown to the screaming girls in the front of the bus. Next went my shirt and V—neck sweater. I, I couldn't do a thing to stop it. I held onto one glow sock and wouldn't let it go. Couldn't stop it. The laughter. The pointing. I tried to cover myself with my hands. It only made them shout louder. Then shout louder, "Tally tallywacker, we can see your tallywacker!"

The arrival at Presidio Junior High prompted a quick exit by everyone. Except me. And Bobby Ensign. He was still sitting in his seat trying to stop a bleeding lip. I curled under the back row of seats naked except for one sock. I was just going to stay there 'til the bus went wherever buses go. Anyplace but here on this first day of school. With kids jumping up and down outside the bus to see what all the commotion was about. To see the 7th grader that was pantsed.

Bobby saved me like he did that time at Kezar. He came to the back of the bus and gave me his sweatshirt and what was left of my white shirt and sweater. I wrapped his sweatshirt around my waist like a skirt. Something is better than nothing. Folded my shirt and sweater and placed them in my torn lunch bag. I threw the orange glow sock under the back seat. I didn't ever want to wear glow socks again. To never draw attention to myself. Never.

I waited for the school bell and gradual exodus of students crowding around the bus. Then Bobby went to the driver and told him to drive us to his father's red brick firehouse on Geary just up from the Cliff House. When the driver refused, Bobby threatened him for allowing his friend to be beat up. I could hear Bobby shouting, "My Dad knows policemen, lots of them!" The driver reluctantly closed the folding door and retraced our path up Geary. We didn't find my pants but Bobby's father had extra clothing. I looked like a fireman with very large black pants held up by loose suspenders. Huge boots, and the best part – a fireman's shirt with a badge.

Bobby's father drove us back to Presidio with lots of advice about 'Don't be afraid, you gotta stand up and fight . . .' Strange thing at Presidio was that the event seemed to be a non-event. The counselors wanted Bobby and I back into our assigned classes. It was the first day of school, a day of confusion. Kids I didn't know asked if I was a real, but short, fireman. Most everyone didn't know where to go or where to find their classes. I'd have to make up a story for my mother about what happened to my new clothes but that was possible.

On the return bus trip, Bobby's father and two other firemen greeted each 8th grade boy as they entered the bus and told them, "Knock it off! Listen, knock it off!" They jabbed each 8th grader with one finger as they spoke. "Got it?" It reminded me of my mother's warning, that there is always someone faster only in this case there is always someone bigger. Like most warnings it fell on deaf ears. Like most warnings it would also come to pass.

HUDSON
CALIFORNIA
JBD 560

SALVATION IS A RED HOT HUDSON

The incident with the rowdies in the back of the bus prompted one of Bobby's greatest solutions to a problem. At first I didn't know what he was talking about. "Look Ron, pirates at sea, if they see an abandoned ship, they can claim it." All the while he's pointing out the window at parked cars along our bus route. "See, there's one!" "What are you talking about?" "Look at the Hudson, just been sitting there, it's abandoned – we can take it, it's the law of the sea!" "You mean steal a car!" "Yes, and ride to school in style." "Great Bobby, but we don't have a drivers' license!" I offered in the voice of reason. Bobby spoke with the voice of sweet revenge. "Do you want to ride in this stupid bus with idiots sitting in the back spitting on us or have your own wheels?" That was an easy question to answer. Bobby and I went about stealing that Hudson automobile that had been sitting and collecting dust for what looked like years. It surely was abandoned, unwanted, and uncared for.

It's easier to steal a car than you think. Oh, you can hotwire it, but it's easier to simply call a tow truck and have your prize delivered to Bobby Ensign's garage on 45th Ave. It was our love machine in waiting. Perfect for picking up girls and driving to Presidio and maybe the El Rancho or Geneva Drive-In Theater.

We went to work on this car I M M E D I A T E L Y ! Body putty and sanding to fill in the bumps and bruises. Moon hubcaps and snap on white walls. Dual glass pack mufflers to give the Hudson a throaty rumble. Rake the chassis by lowering the front and lifting the back. Paint 'cat eyes' over the front headlights. Yes, it was looking cool.

Unlike me, Bobby was skilled with his hands and his basement was crammed with remnants of our radio project and the tools for tearing down and building this dream machine. We returned to our golf business to raise the $120 needed for a Mission District Tijuana tuck and roll blue vinyl interior. The final touch was to paint our car Candy Apple Lipstick Red. The body, wheel wells, and dashboard looked so great that we decided to paint inside the trunk and engine. We spray painted the inside of the hood then the block, spark plugs, water pump, battery, carburetor, and even the radiator - everything Candy Apple Lipstick Red. I mean if girls looked under the hood we wanted them to be impressed. This car was HOT!!!

We hung a pair of fuzzy dice on the rearview mirror and checked out the radio. The far end of the dial, we were ready. It had taken us 6 weeks of hard everyday work but it was worth it. Every bus ride to Presidio and back we dreamed out loud about our freedom and our Hudson. Dreams are the one thing no one can take away.

Bobby let me do the honors of backing the Hudson out of the garage. I could barely see over the steering wheel and only my toes pressed against the clutch and accelerator. Bobby Ensign's father and one of his friends had gathered to watch the unveiling. I touched the fuzzy dice for luck and turned on the ignition. Then hit the gas with a delicate tap of my right foot. Put the gear stick in reverse and slowly let out the clutch. The car quietly slid down the driveway with rear tires gently touching the uplift of the street. Bobby Ensign father and the man standing next to him broke out in applause.

I thought it was a salute of some kind so I slipped the gear stick back into neutral and hit the gas as hard as I could. BANG!!!! Black smoke went pouring out our dual glass pack mufflers. And the front hood exploded upward. The engine was on fire! Not a little fire but a major blaze. I guess we had used the wrong paint or maybe should not have painted the engine. The fire quickly became a bellowing black smoke that smelled like burning rubber.

"Get out of there!" Bobby Ensign's father yelled. I was quick to oblige. Bobby and I didn't know what to do as Bobby's father grabbed a fire extinguisher from the garage and damped the fire and our dreams. All the while, yelling at us, "You dumb shits, do you know who this is?" As he turned he sprayed his friend with foam – "This is the San Francisco Police Chief – we've been watchin' you and waitin' for it all to get fixed up – now – now this – you dumb stupid shits!" "You stole the police chief's car!"

With that revelation Bobby and I started running with a fireman and a police chief close behind. They chased us all the way down 45th Ave. 'til they ran out of breath on Noriega Street. It probably wasn't a good idea to give the police chief the finger and a final, "It's our car, we fixed it up, we found it, no one wanted it, and it's ours . . ."

Sometimes my mouth gets ahead of my feet. With the old men holding their sides and walking slowly back to Bobby's house and the smoldering car, we noticed a new kid on the block. He had run along side of us laughing at the exchange of words in the ensuing chase. And boxing the air. Keeping pace with us, sometimes running back- ward egging us to run faster, to keep up with him.

His name was Sam Rivera. He had a pleasant way of saying hello that didn't match his body. He was bigger than Bobby but different. Slim and powerful with tattoos cov- ering both arms. No one in the Sunset had tattoos. His skin was a sandy bronze and his hair was short and frizzy. And that smile. It was infectious.

He and his father had just moved onto 45th Ave. and he'd been watching us work on the Hudson. He liked our car and agreed it should be ours. We talked about the bus to Presidio and our problems with older boys. Again he just smiled. He was going to be in our class at Presidio. Would be taking the bus on Monday. And oh yes, his father was a professional boxer. He threw several punches in the air and did that stutter step he had done running along side of us, "Dad's a boxer like me, yes."

Yes!

On Monday I took my customary seat next to the window with Bobby squeezed next to me and Sam Rivera from Puerto Rico sitting on the aisle. When we heard the familiar taunt, Bobby just grinned. "Dirty Lil, dirty Lil, lives on top of garbage hill, never washes..." The older boys rushed down the aisle toward the new kid on the bus – Sam Rivera from Puerto Rico.

Mistake!

There was a lightning flurry of blows as Sam's fist smashed into noses and soft bellies. It took only a few seconds.

Now we sit in the back of the bus. Me and my gang looking for a car to steal. You can't have a gang with one short kid and his best friend Bobby that doesn't like to fight. But, with Bobby and I sitting in the back of the bus with our friend Sam Rivera from Puerto Rico – well – that's a gang.

It's then that the thought crossed my mind. A simple thought. A song sung from the back of the bus. 'Dirty Lil, dirty Lil' it hung there like a dark cloud. I looked at Bobby and Sam Rivera. We never did sing that ditty. There was no reason. No reason at all to spit on anyone. Or taunt someone that was different. We were going to junior high and there would be girls there with tight sweaters and sweet smiles.

Mom's basement dance studio

Ron # 4

<u>AT THE END OF THE LINE</u>

At Presidio I figured the only way to have friends and be in the 'in' crowd was to play basketball. When classmates asked what I did I would answer, "Oh, play a little ball, you know, basketball." There wasn't much interest in track and everyone talked about basketball and attending the games against other junior highs. Besides with my speed, basketball was the one thing I was good at. So I spent every Saturday at Francis Scott Key on Kirkham playing basketball. I had a quick first step and could drive to my right for a hook shot against even the taller high school players that hung out at the 'Key'. I loved getting to the playground early. The smell of spoiled milk in the playground air. Fantasy shots falling into the basket following a mythical last second count down. Game winning jump shots or drives to the basket. The only break being a cherry coke at the fountain pharmacy on Lawton.

Playgrounds in the 50's had directors that organized competitive games with other playgrounds. So we would play pick up games against West Sunset or Big Rec with uniforms and referees. It was a great mixing ground to meet players from all over the city. We'd play against the Buchanan Y and Chinese Y. We got to know each other by name and reputation. In the future, we would all be on the high school teams in our neighborhood.

I made charts to record how many hours I was practicing dribbling with my left hand and percentage of free throws made for every 100 attempts. I marked places on the playground basketball court and took 100 shots from each spot before leaving the yard. This is my home. This court. This is where I belong. This is where I will triumph and have teammates and friends to share this love affair with a game called basketball.

Bobby wasn't one for the dusty work and dedication I was demanding. He was tall but rather goofish when it came to organized sport. Girls started to be attracted to his Robert Mitchum look and he found a calling in the Boy Scouts. He was always busy making a merit badge project in his garage. Some feathery thing or ceramic bowl or just tramping off to Mt. Tamalpais with Sam Rivera to drink beer. I was busy shooting free throws and dreaming of glory.

I was more than excited when 'tryouts for the boy's basketball team' was posted on the gym wall at Presidio Jr. High. This is the moment I had waited for and planned for. The tryout was for 6:00 in the evening so I had to have my Mom drive me over and wait outside. Here it was at last. Being at school after everyone had gone home. Just me and other basketball players sharing this secret time and pleasure. I love everything about basketball. The sound of the ball like a drum against the wooden floor. The squeal of shoes dancing against shouts of "block out" – "I've got it" – Bodies pushing and shoving for position. The ball hanging on the rim to tantalize the shooter or expectant rebound. Clamor of "Good shot!" "I'll take it out."

In preparation for this moment my mother had bought me a new pair of All Star Keds. White high tops with a red star on the side. To stand out I wore my basketball uniform top from Sunset playground with my lucky number 12. Mom waited outside as I entered the sweaty smell of a gym. Vapor eyes smiled down upon the floor causing it to glow like a promise.

There were about 30 kids trying out for the team. The coach came out and spilled onto the floor a dozen basketballs. There was this mad rush to get a ball and dribble to the nearest hoop to launch a shot. I watched each player very carefully. You can tell the players. It's how they release the ball for a jump shot. Their balance. How they square up to the face the basket. The shooting elbow in close to the body. The release of the ball with finger tips giving the ball a gently reverse spin. The follow through. Concentration on the rim. And lay ups. Those kids that jump off the wrong foot or can't place the ball softly against the magic square on the backboard. It was all there in front of me. I counted four or five players with athletic skill and a few wide bodies for rebounding and control of the backboard.

I was surprised when the coach reappeared from his office and blew his whistle. Then shouted, "All balls to the corner of the gym and into the ball rack!" With a second shrill whistle we were told to take a stand on the half court line facing him. "All right, everyone, I want one line tallest to shortest. Come on, get with it. Tallest this end of the line, shortest to that end!" As he pointed we all raced to take our respective place. I was almost at the very end of shortest players. Two Chinese kids I knew to be good players took their place at my end of the line up.

My heart was pounding and my hands were perspiring. But now it would begin. The tryout. There would be speed dribble drills with both hands. And chances to mark the wall with your vertical leap. We would have a lay up drill where those who could shoot with both hands would excel. And hopefully a scrimmage where court savvy, passing, and use of screens and defense would be evident. I secretly smiled. Couldn't wait to get into a scrimmage and show my speed and court vision. We were standing in line like horses getting ready for a great race.

Following a loud blast of his whistle the coach approached our line up. He started with the tallest boys as he explained our tryout. "All right you, you and" he pointed to the tallest boy and the next tallest boy down the line. There wasn't much difference in size. He gave each boy a number – "Number 1, 2, 3, 4" and then stopped at 12. "You 12 are on the team, the rest of you can go."

When Mom asked how the tryout went I didn't answer. What do you say to a dream taken away by some asshole coach? I hated Presidio. It was like a jail. Long rows of putrid green lockers. Crowds of students scurrying from class to class. Everyone having some place to go. Someone to meet. They would walk past me like I didn't exist. There was no time for kickball or folk dancing. So far away from home on 46th Ave. No chance to just run home for lunch to share a sandwich with Mom or Glenna. Even the trumpet betrayed me.

Like my father I could play anything written down on a sheet of music. The last period of the day at Presidio was band with Mr. Peel. Powerhouse was in this class pounding away on a snare drum. It was pretty chaotic. Mr. Peel passed out music sheets to each instrumental group. It was a Sousa March. Easy enough to play as first horn. To add to the cacophony I triple tongued into the march. Mr. Peel nodded approval. He knew T.C. The trumpet player next to me looked at the music but riffed into a jazz like counterpoint to what was written. I had never heard something so original and beautiful. So filled with

emotion – soul. He made the written notes dance and sing. When I asked him where
he saw or found those notes, he just pointed to his head. "In here." I put my horn in
its case. I wouldn't pick up a trumpet again until high school – but that's a story still to
come. I felt I didn't fit in, anyplace. The English and history classes at Presidio were the
memorization of events and people I didn't care about. I stopped paying attention and
started looking out the window at the daily visits of fog like ghosts.

In sheet metal shop I made a dustpan. I should be good at sheet metal. My grandfather
on my father's side of the family had a sheet metal business in Fallon, Nevada. T.C. told
me his father was the first mayor of Fallon and the town drunk. Made sheet metal water
tanks and bins for agricultural use. Bobby Ensign's dustpan was much better than mine.
Of course, it was a merit badge project.

Mine had droplets of solder. Red-hot solder that accidentally splashed on the dustpan
handle and on my hand. Then not so accidentally red-hot solder found its way to tiny
pinpoints of pain on my arm. Like grey pearls. I thought I deserved the pain. Something
was wrong with me. I needed to feel something. Anything. Wanted more and more, just
to be alone.

<u>SUTRO BATHS</u>

Some days I just walked away from Presidio. No one noticed or cared. I'd take all after-noon to walk home. My daily stop was Sutro Baths. This grand palace with a Victorian staircase leading downward to a museum of the strange and exotic. There was an ice skating rink and pools on the lower levels but I lingered in the museum. I was usually alone in this cavernous space that heated up in the afternoon like a tropic hot house. Large ferns stretched toward the glass canopy. Some of this glass was broken giving the appearance of a mouth with broken teeth.

If you listened carefully you cold hear the ocean wave whispering below you. And if you paid attention the exhibits before you would speak to your loneliness and need for companionship. The life size naked Japanese sculpture stared forever forward, every tiny hair and muscle on his body forbidden from movement. Trapped like me in the place of freaks. Tiny Thumb and his miniature wife in a stagecoach going nowhere. Skeletons of giant reptiles and African masks that told of torment and death. Great toothpick creations that replicated amusement parks that no longer existed. A mechanical fortune teller that followed you with her eyes.

Often I would finish my tour of the unusual by gong down two flights of stairs to the Sutro Baths. For 10 cents I'd be given a woolen black bathing suit that itched and a small while towel. The changing rooms were cabanas built into the side of the cliff. The pool itself consisted of a large rectangular plunge with slides and suspended rings and flying trapeze bars. Above this large pool that braced against large windows and sounds of the ocean was a diving pool. And along the gallery facing these pools were three small pools with differing temperature from cold to hot. Each of these small pools had a raft in the middle. On weekdays I was one of only a few people using the pool. I'd lie in the warm salted water and look into the glass domed ceiling. The salt in the water would allow me to effortlessly float. A tropic heat and smell of sulpher surrounded me. Condensation would grip the wooden rafters and fall about me like gentle tears. Drop after drop. Drop. Drop. I liked floating in the warm water. Being alone. Crying

In this watery retreat I would close my eyes and imagine digging up grandpa's gun and shooting those 8th grade boys that had hurt me. I'd shoot them right between the eyes. Take away their smile. To make them forever stand still like those creatures in the museum. To be a warning for all those passing by about what can happen when you make fun of someone.

ENTRANCE TO
LADIES' DRESSING ROOMS
PANORAMA OF THE WORLD
A TOUR OF THE
IN TEN MINUTES

THE FULL MOON THAT NEVER CHANGED

Everything seemed to be changing. Karl closed his grocery store. Safeway opened across the street and took his customers with their temporary cheap prices and abundance of produce. A freezer filled with the latest frozen TV dinners. Both bakeries kitty corner from Karl's closed their doors when Safeway introduced Wonder Bread – a white bread that you could squeeze in your fingers like Elmer's glue. The kids that used to play in the street were now at home watching the first televisions. Grandpa Pop had a stroke. My mother never forgave Mt. Zion Hospital for their poor care and the theft of his diamond ring.

Pop spent most of his days sitting in a large cushioned chair with a robe covering the paralyzed side of his body. I'd often visit and sit on the floor in front of him and softly loop a tennis ball into the crook of his good arm. He'd grab the ball if he could or let it roll down his body to the floor. I would do this for hours and watch his contorted mouth trying to smile or say a labored "good boy". This reminded me of the enjoyment I got slamming a ball against the stairs and trying to catch an unexpected bounce or fly. To keep our game lively, I'd often recite the plays of an entire Seals game. "Runner on first, deep drive to right field . . ." The Seals were on television every weekend playing the Oakland Oaks or Seattle Rainiers and roller derby with Ann Calvello and the Bay Bombers along with wrestling were his viewing favorites.

When he passed away, Grandma and her red turban hat moved in with us. Grandma and I had always been best of friends. Her name was Grace. It fit her. She was always taking care of someone on the phone or going into the opium dens next to Pop's President Follies to help someone get home. She held court at her kitchen table for the odd assortment of dancers and wrestlers brought home by Pop. She taught me how to play poker or sit in the kitchen and kibitz with visitors. Particularly Willie Acker with his vacant stares and adams apple that moved like a barometer to his thoughts. She would translate for this man that stood like a telephone pole about his being with Macarthur and the landing in the Philippines. How it was all a set up for the press. Him wading ashore. And why he had given me that RCA radio to listen to the world. All three San Francisco daily newspapers, the Call Bulletin, Examiner, and the Chronicle all had headlines about war in Korea and Macarthur wanting to use the atomic bomb. Will and Grandma never trusted the news. Hated war.

With Grandma I read my first books. The Knife about what happened to an indigenous culture when a steel blade changed everything. And a book about elephants. How they circle to protect the vulnerable or baby members of their group. Their affection and loyalty to each other. Capacity to silently move mountains and swim great distances. Stories of her family coming across the county in a covered wagon. Her homestead in Oregon's Willamette Valley that my mother took us to visit. The root cellar was still there. And the hand pump to bring water.

Grandma with a turban hat and me with the sailor hat next to mom.

Grandma shared a living history with me in the form of a stereopticon. A sliding wood frame that carried two adjacent sepia photos that when seen through a viewfinder would become three - dimensional images of the 1906 earthquake and fire in San Francisco. She was here as a nurse. But the most interesting thing we talked about was basketball. As a woman in the Oregon schools she played in a game where women wore bloomers and were only allowed to take three dribbles before passing. They were not allowed to run and stood as offensive or defensive players in their respective court. She told me of Japanese friends forcibly taken away and imprisoned to stay on their side of the fence. I told her about Bobby and I trying to communicate with the Russians and our search for a Japanese miniature submarine in a cave beneath the Cliff House. She was the only one I told about the bus ride to Presidio. I guess I didn't realize it at the time but we were always discussing the pain and revelation that comes from change. Freedom. Believing in oneself and finding love all around you.

So it was hard for me when Grandma became ill and moved in with us. She spent most days sitting in the kitchen smoking Chesterfields and watching coffee percolate on the stove. Spending countless hours ironing long strands of tinsel in preparation for the coming Christmas tree decoration. Enjoying her weekly trips to a séance reader in West Portal to talk to Pop. And her nightly call to me – to come and sit on the end of her bed and look at the moon. "Look Ronald a full moon, it's good luck." We would sit there quietly night after night looking at the full moon that never changed. It was the street lamp across the street on Kirkham.

Grandma's homestead in Oregon 1946

Grandma

Doug, Grandma, Mom, me and T.C.

The Hot House Ocean Beach

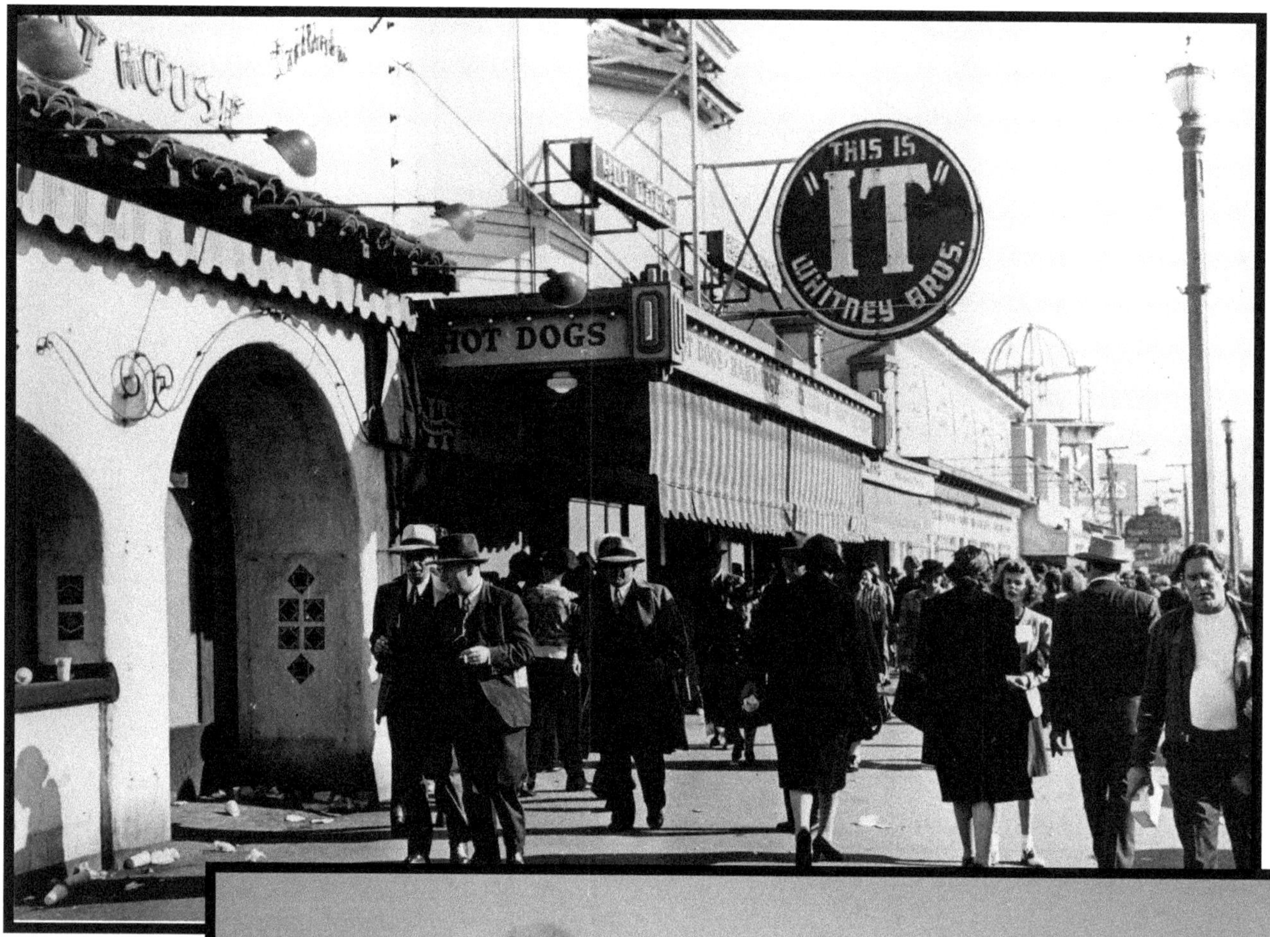

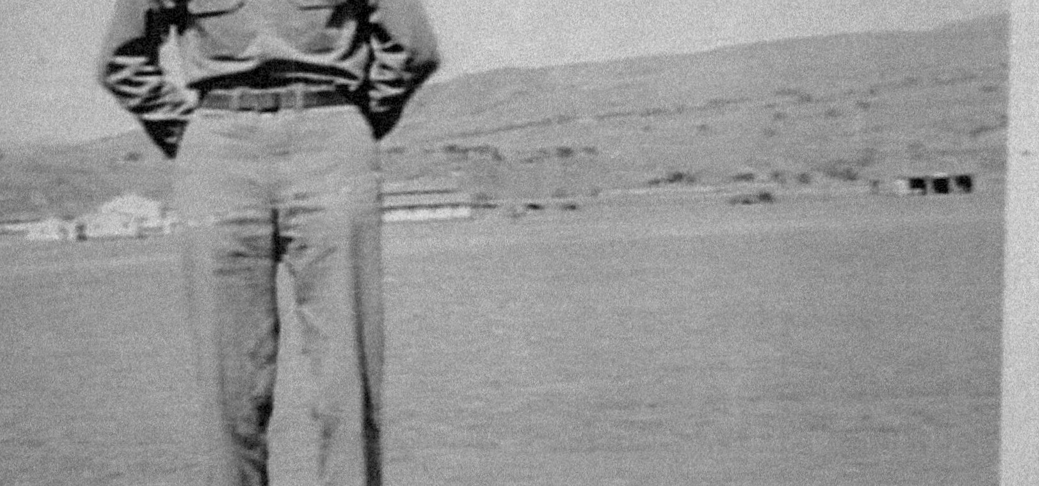

Willie Acker

I'M A LEAVIN' NOW

When Grandma died I felt more alone than ever. My brother Doug was five years younger. That's a large gap. He and his friend Alfredo were busy taking apart my flexy and building scooters to slide down the Kirkham hill. Or just getting into mischief. One fourth of July they made a bomb that blew a hole in the outside of the garage and set the house afire. I filled the upstairs tub and ferried pots of water to put out the blaze. Truth is I panicked! There was a garden hose three feet from the fire. Glenna was the only one that always seemed to know how we were feeling. She was psychic. Did healings on the phone for her friends in the Bahai Faith and took us to flying saucer conventions. She's the reason I mysteriously went to Stanford but that's another story.

Sandy and Jean were alienated loners like me. They had been separated from their friends in South San Francisco and lost in city schools. Sandy with his Mick Jagger lips and red carrot hair was a wonderful artist. He taught himself to play piano on the upright sitting in the living room. Jean was gawky and wore glasses that scared away boys and clicky girl companions. T.C. was starting to drink beer on the weekends. I, my brother, Sandy and Jean were no longer the children he'd organized to clean the garage or take bike rides to Sutro Park above the Cliff House. Or spend an afternoon helping him wax the car with Johnson's Car Wax. Oh, he still drove to the beach to play his horn to a dieing sun. And then to the Hot House at Playland for enchiladas. And sometimes we'd go to San Remo's Restaurant in North Beach for a home style Italian Dinner. One dollar and fifty cents for a pre - determined meal of salad, raviolis, main course and cup of vanilla ice cream for your espresso coffee.

Within this hubbub of events even T.C., the happiest person I ever knew, was showing signs of desperation. His shoes, for the first time in my memory were going unshined. He was working what he called his "day to day job" selling TVs and appliances at Sterling Furniture on Market Street. Mom and I were no longer going to Sweets with my Dad to see a movie and then dance in that swirl of moving bodies before driving home with T.C. One afternoon I found my father passed out drunk in the hallway. T.C.'s favorite 78 recording of Count Basie was playing on the hallway console. The final melody played out and the needle was skipping, trying to start over again. This would become a regular event.

Mom still organized elaborate Christmas parties for the family but there were no longer neighbors or local merchants in attendance. And we all missed Grandma, Pop and Willie Acker. With Grandma's passing Willie told us in a clear Southern drawl, "I'm a leavin' now!" We never saw him again.

Glenna and Mom stopped teaching ballroom lessons in the basement and took a summer job as hamburger cooks at the Ben Lomond Town and Country Lodge. A summer job away from the city and the cement like fog. This allowed us to buy a small summer cabin in Ben Lomond. For the first time in my life I was about to spend summer in the sunshine. My Dad named the place, "Ronnie's Doug Out!" My life was about to be rocked by a girl named Kay Casselli.

COOL AND THE BIG IT!

Summer 1955. I just wanted to be cool. Everything is changing. Even the music. At the far end of the dial KSFO in San Francisco playing the hit parade. At the top of the chart, "Shrimp boats are a comin' their sails are in sight, you better hurry, hurry, hurry home – " Farther down the dial "Shboom a lone ding dong a lang a lang a lang boom ba do a do a do ba da . . ." by the White Boys – but further down the dial, "I found my thrillll on blueberry hill" by Fats Domino. And that was COOL!

Street conversation between Bobby, Sam Rivera from Puerto Rico and I was about hard ons and heat ons. Now I wasn't sure what a hard on or heat on meant but I had ways of changing the conversation. "Bobby this is a mixed drink – ginger ale and now you add the secret ingredient – vanilla extract, that's the alcohol content – and mint jam – that gives it a kick! Think of it as a merit badge in alcohol consumption." And Ron's real zorch sun tan oil. "Baby oil and a splash of iodine, then you mix in the mint jam. Yea, I know we look a little green layin' out here in the sun, but girls will notice us, I think."

Attracting girls was important if you wanted to be cool. And being cool was associated with your hair. We went from slick comb backs with a part on one side, or buzz cut, to a converging curl that comes from the side of your hair to the front. This curl kinda dangled on your forehead. Like an antenna or something. It meant that you were tough and ready for the 'Big It!!' Now I wasn't really sure what the 'Big It' was but I knew it had to do with girls and being cool.

My first experience of 'Doing It' was in Ben Lomond, at the weekly summer dance held at the dam. In the 50's every working class family I knew had a summer place to get away from the fog that covered the Sunset like a wet coffin. Most of the Catholic families and particularly the firemen and policemen of the city went to Rio Nido on the Russian River. Wealthier families had summer homes at Lake Tahoe. And all the rest of us headed for the sun in Santa Cruz and the towns along the San Lorenzo River – Felton, Ben Lomond and Boulder Creek.

My Mom found us a little cabin in Ben Lomond. It was located in what once was a training camp for fighters. The cabin had one living room large enough to fit a couch that would open into a bed. A bedroom next to the cabin's bathroom, kitchen and dining room. And a small screened in porch. Painted red, white and blue, it was like an American flag among the redwood trees. I think my mother chose this place because it was built over a creek. Being a romantic she enjoyed the trickling of water under the cabin and the trees whose tops turned in the afternoon breeze. Her first improvement to her dream was a wood-burning fireplace. Of course in the winter rains, before our first summer at the cabin, the underpinning for the fireplace clogged the creek. The cabin collapsed in a V shape into a now, rather widened creek.

Undaunted my mother hired local carpenters to lift the debris out of the creek and build a huge deck to span the enlarged creek. The tiny cabin now had a deck that rivaled an aircraft carrier with a fireplace. And T.C.'s renewed sign, 'Ronnie's Doug Out #2'.

The beauty of this winged cabin is that Mom and Glenna could invite the world to stay with us. And they did. Aunts and Uncles. Cousins. Friends of Sandy and Jean from South San Francisco. On one weekend I counted 23 people sleeping on decks and under the trees. Mornings were spent with Mom and Glenna making pancakes for the horde. Evenings were filled with board games, charades and costume plays usually directed by Sandy. On weekends, T.C. and some of his music friends would join us to toot their horns and drink beer. It was simply impossible to feel alone or depressed in this time and place called summer vacation.

During the days, Mom and Glenna worked at the Town and Country Pool Hamburger Stand while I spent my time trying to ditch my younger brother and meet the teenage boys, Sunny and Skip Sundberg, that lived across the creek and wooden plank that bounced when you crossed it. Skip was portly while Sunny was skinny. Both sang in the San Francisco Boy's Chorus. We started out without saying a word. Throwing rocks into the San Lorenzo. Then hanging out in Ben Lomond next to the dam. To sit and comb our hair. Then jump into the frigid dammed up river and shake our wet hair at sun bathing girls.

Somehow the Sundbergs had met Ray Haight from Balboa High School. Ray was short like me but with an 'I got you' smile and perfect hair. He had the Elvis curl up front and down the back a DA Ducks Ass cool. Ray's best friend, Jerry Granelli, joined us. He was a drummer, already playing gigs at Club Verdi, and wherever he went he had these drumsticks. Even on the beach at the dam, he had these sticks pounding metal trashcans or sticking out the back of his bathing suit like a wooden tail. I noticed that girls' eyes followed Jerry wherever he went. And he knew it!

Every night at the dam there was a planned activity. Movie night. Square dancing. Nature movies . . .but the big event for teens was dance night. It was on Friday. The pavilion was decorated by strings of colored lights that seemed to glow with hope. I sat with Granelli, Skip and Sunny along with Ray Haight on our familiar perch – the railing at the entrance to the dance floor. 45's played over the loudspeakers as teens poured onto the cement dance floor. Girls swished past us with their moving skirts and hair that smelled of shampoo. Always giggling. Sometimes dancing with each other and flirting with the older hard looking boys. Boys with leather jackets and scowls. I was wearing a yellow McGregor. I wished I could scowl.

That's when it happened. She just walked right up to me and asked, "Can you do the dirty bop?" Jerry Granelli started clicking his drum sticks against the wood railing. Sunny, Skip and Ray looked at each other and then at me. Their eyes widened with transparent questions, 'What's going on here?' 'Some kinda trick maybe.' 'She's going to make fun of you and us.' She studied their stares. Then looked right at them. And asked, "Can you do the dirty bop?"

Oh, feet don't fail me now! I slide off my rail seat and stood in front of her. She was beautiful. Spanish eyes and a dark brown tan. Well endowed. 'God she's well endowed.' Standing there I realized she's also a little bit taller than I am. But then most girls are. No, she's a lot taller!

She's wearing a pink sweater with these tiny cotton balls that jiggle as she starts to turn and walk away. It's now or never. This isn't the waltz, fox trot or tango I learned in Mom's dance class but movement that conveys feeling. Lust! My voice cracks, "Yea – uhm I can do the dirty dirty!" My feet start doing a version of the Charleston. My hands are into the Hokey Pokey. Hips trying to gyrate when she smiled and joined my dance of love. "I knew you could dance, most boys can't dance – my name's Kay Casselli."

"That's my sister over there, Marge," A gaggle of girls pointed toward us. Maybe this was some kind of cruel joke. Granelli, Sunny, Skip and Ray just looked aghast. Then a slow record dropped into play – Moonglow. She takes both my hands and pulls them around her waist then drops her arms over my shoulders. I am slow dancing with Kay Casselli and no one is laughing. OK, she's just a little taller than I thought. My head rests on the top of her breasts. And we are swaying side to side. I'm in love.

We're a match made in heaven. I mean, we like the same things. Cherry coke at the corner soda fountain, Canasta, and Milk Duds chewed with Juicy Fruit gum. Kay Casselli and her sister Marge, that looked like the movie star Doris Day, had a summer place behind the Ben Lomond Town and Country and around the corner from Skip and Sunny's. And they had a pool. I think it was Marge and the pool that attracted a new kid Johnny Weissmuller Jr., who was tall and gangly and looked just like his father. He needed a safe place to hangout. He was always being bullied and chased around Ben Lomond by older boys that wanted to make a name for themselves by saying they beat up Tarzan. We sure were an odd mix but we were friends. Enjoying a summer of card playing, swimming, and romance.

I loved watching Kay dive into the pool and gracefully swim a length or chase after Granneli who was hitting the pool sides with drumsticks. Kay's mother always sat motionless behind dark sunglasses at the end of the pool watching Johnny Weissmuller bounce on the diving board before knifing into the water. Evenings were spent at the Casselli's dancing to the latest rhythm and blues and playing Canasta with friends invited into our in-group. This is the summer I would never forget. This is the summer I would do the 'Big It.'

Of course to do the 'Big It' you have to have a plan – be cool – and solve the hair problem. The plan was simple. I'd present Kay Casselli the red track pin given to me by Bobby Ensign. This pin and its red ribbon for track would mean we are 'going steady'. And steady would lead to 'feel ups' and the 'Big It'. To be cool I'd roll up the sleeves of my shirt along with the back collar and put a roll of gym socks in the heel of my shoes. Taller and cooler. The hair problem would require a complete makeover. To form that converging curl over my forehead and DA Duck's Ass in the back, I needed help. Dixie Peach Pomade, Elmer's White Glue, and mint jam – of course you mix it! Sticking this concoction to my hair took several hours – but it was worth it. I mean Jerry Granelli and Marge Casselli had already done it! Yea, yea, yea, he stole a Nash rambler and drove her to the dump. When they came back he was hitting everything in sight with his sticks and she was smiling. A smile that told you she had done it for sure. Now it's my turn! Put my plan in motion.

I'm with Kay Casselli – her folks are out – Moonglow's playing on the record player. She's chewing Juicy Fruit gum with Milk Duds and wearing a white angora sweater that looks like cotton candy. We're playing Canasta and I'm looking for the right moment. Oh jeez, Jerry and Marge are on the patio swing and he's getting a hickey. I'd do anything to get a hickey!

All right, all right, put my plan in motion. I ask Kay, "Would you, you know, like to go steady?" She says, "Yes." I go to give her my track pin but stick myself. I'm sucking my bleeding finger as she places the pin on her sweater above her heart all the while whispering, "Yes, I'll go steady with you – yes." Holy Mackerel! She's rolling up the bottom of her sweater exposing two tan lined white breasts held tightly in a lacey white bra. 'Vava Voom!' I had never seen a real life bra. Two breasts being held in suspension like two eggs over easy.

I've got to get that bra off. I reach behind Kay. 'OK, OK, stay calm, it's easy, a switch or something maybe like a belt buckle. I can feel the clasp. Just pull it off. OK, OK that doesn't work. Twist, twist it like a bottle cap, yank it, no, no, it's not working forget the back, I'll just bite off this strap in the front of the bra that separates me from Holy Glory!'

I plunge down head first between her breasts and start biting away at the bra. Chewing. Back and forth. Up and down. Pulling with all my might, teeth interlocked with fabric. Huh huh huh – 'What's she doing? Holding Canasta cards in one hand and pulling up her sweater with the other.' Nothing can stop me now! Harder. Faster – when I suddenly realize – 'Oh God – my hair – my hair is stuck to her white angora sweater. And I've got a hard on! That's what a hard on is – .' I'm desperately trying to free my hair from her sweater with one hand and cover up my hard on with the other when she yells, "Canasta!"

This isn't what I expected for the 'Big It'. I had pricked my finger. Lost one shoe in all the excitement. And swallowed my gum! I waddled home. Fell in the creek. A thousand mosquitoes attached themselves to my hair.

Lying in the screened porch bed next to the radio listening to Blue Berry Hill my Mom comes in to say goodnight. I tried to explain why I lost my shoe, the mosquitoes, and how hard it is to go steady. She just pulled up the blankets to tuck me in. Then quite matter of factly whispered, "There will be lots of nights like this." "I hope not Mom, I really hope not." But alone, on this warm summer night, just being there listening to the radio I thought to myself. 'I should go out and buy a bra and find out how it works and I can tell Bobby and everyone – and you know for a moment, before I swallowed my gum – yea, I was cool.

Kay, Ron, Marge and Granelli

VOLUNTEERS
1954
A. P. Giannini
Basketball Team - 1954

KINGS OF THE HILL

Things were dramatically improving in my life. I had a secret summer life with good friends that played out in love letters and subsequent summers. Even junior high improved as we became the first class to attend Giannini Jr. High in the Sunset. The basketball coach Barney Greenberg accepted the shortest ninth grader as ball manager. All right, all right I got to practice with the team and travel with the team. I was with my friends Bobby Ensign, Sam Rivera from Puerto Rico, and Michael 'Powerhouse' Hancock. And I was looking forward to entering Lincoln High School. High on a hilltop in the Sunset District.

Bobby Ensign, my Mom, Sam Rivera and me on our way to Lincoln High School

THE UNEXPECTED

I wasn't expecting the saddest news of all time. It was the end of summer. Sam Rivera from Puerto Rico drown while surfing off the coast at Pacifica. How could this happen? And why? Sam is buried in the US cemetery in South San Francisco. I think about him every time I drive down 280 past row upon row of white crosses. He was the kindest and strongest man I every knew. Life isn't fair. We are a brief spark in a bonfire of time. We want to impose reason or faith upon our life. How absurd.

Sometimes life can't be planned or explained, only appreciated. That's how my life with Deanna began. We were juniors at Lincoln High School. When I first saw her she was all wet. Her blouse clung to her body exposing her bra. Yes, there's that bra thing again. She was laughing. Then pointing angrily at the boys that had thrown her into Fleischhaker Pool. Her photo was in the local newspaper. That wet hair and surprised look at being pushed into the cold water. Those green eyes that spoke of embarrassed joy. I liked her from the first time I saw her. That ponytail and the way she sat with one leg curled underneath her. Easy to talk with. To just sit on her parents couch and watch American Bandstand and Soul Train. Waiting for her brother and parents to go to bed. The ease in which she welcomed my touch. Making out to the closing test pattern of Channel 5. And conspiring into the night. Sneaking into El Rancho Drive-In and watching submarine races at "the circle". The 'Y' dances. Poetry at the Spaghetti Factory and crowding behind chicken wire to hear comedians and singers at the Hungry I. Late night swing dancing at Club New Yorker and ice cream sundaes at Mel's and the Hippo. Only one of our conspiracies turned out not as expected! It would be a great surprise for my mother.

Bright yellow like the sun. My mother would love it. No, I had never painted a kitchen before, but I could do it! Mom and Dad are down in Disneyland with my brother. I told them I was too old for Disney. Perfect. They'd be gone for the weekend. Two days. The house to myself. And my plan to surprise my mother. I'd paint her kitchen bright Sun Flower Yellow!

The hardware store on Judah provided the paint. I didn't know how much I'd need, but 2 gallons seemed right. "Brushes or rollers?" Uhm - I bought two brushes, one wide and one skinny. A pan and one roller. That's what the hardware store owner said I'd need. I almost forgot the turpentine for clean up. I hadn't thought much about clean up. Just the smile on my mother's face as she surveyed her freshly painted kitchen. This house on 46th Ave. in the Sunset and this kitchen was her pride and joy.

The good thing about this surprise is that I wouldn't be alone. I invited Deanna my high school date for the senior prom to join me. Even gave her a gardenia corsage. You can't paint without a little romance. It was 10 in the morning and we could begin. It would be easy and fast with two painters listening to the Righteous Brothers. The first can of paint was stubborn. I tried a can opener and finally a kitchen knife to pry off the lid. The paint was globular as I spilled it into the pan.

I assumed thickness was goodness. I mean it would cover in one thick yellow coat. I started on the drawer under the sink. Deanna joined me using two brushes to slather paint over the closed cabinet drawers. We were careful to catch the rivulets of yellow before they reached the floor. For the walls and ceiling we used the roller. Swatches of yellow ribbons covered the faded green. I couldn't reach all the way behind the stove but figured no one ever looks back there. The ceiling over the refrigerator was a problem. Splatters of yellow spun off the roller and polka dotted the white enamel fridge. Decision time.

The yellow polka dots streaked when attacked by a moving cloth or towel. You can't have a streaked refrigerator. Solution. Paint it yellow. Yea, it looks a lot better. And that solution applied to drips down the back porch and stairs. And then in the dinette area next to the kitchen. The table and chairs. And every light fixture, some of Mom's good towels and a few plates and glasses. Everything Sun Flower Yellow. She's going to love this color.

It took two days and 4 more gallons of unstirred paint, but finally the job was complete. It just needed one more welcoming touch. The perfect compliment to a new yellow kitchen. I went to the hardware store and purchased a serving tray on wheels. Placing it in the center of the kitchen, I attached a large red ribbon and awaited my mother's approval.

Upon hearing the garage door close, my brother was the first one up the stairs. He ran past the kitchen twice before entering the yellow room. Then escaped to our bedroom yelping, "Who put these yellow finger prints on my Hopalong mug?" Before I could answer T.C. and my Mom were standing and staring at the bright yellow kitchen and the tray with the red ribbon. My father was crying and trying not to laugh. I've only seen my father cry twice. Once standing in front of this beautiful kitchen and the day I left to join Deanna in Alaska.

My mother didn't say a word. Or answer my hopeful question. "Do you like it? And the cart there, you can use it to serve food and stuff, Deanna helped me, it's uhm a surprise, I hope you like it. I could have chosen Egg Blue or Ocean Spray Green but I like..it's Sun Flower Yellow! Your favorite color."

She turned and walked quietly to the back bedroom. I heard the door close and my father's muffled laughter. Then silence. A long silence. The next morning my mother placed our home on 46th Ave. up for sale. She had a new plan for the family. Like so many before us, we would move to a big new track home in San Bruno. Everyone would have their own room. The new house under construction allowed my mother to choose finishes and color. She chose for her kitchen a bright yellow wallpaper with chickens. In pointing out her barnyard motif, she reminded me in no uncertain terms, "Ronald, do not go near a paint brush!" I agreed, "Mom this looks a lot, a lot better." It was our only conversation about the yellow kitchen on 46th Ave. Then she gave me a hug and wouldn't let go. I didn't understand why she couldn't stop crying. Holding onto me and crying.

In moving I discovered my mother kept every report card, art project, Halloween costume, notes and letters and even that sheet metal dust pan with the solder droplets. She had a cardboard box full of family photos that she wouldn't let anyone else carry. There were black and white photos of me playing basketball at Kezar Pavilion. I never knew she was there. Our whole family history of life in the sunset was there, carefully wrapped in her hair ribbons.

Another box was full of photo albums. Black and White photos of the dancers and musicians she and T.C. had known from their days at the Fox Theater on Market Street. The same photos that had graced the walls of her and Glenna's knotty pine dance studio in

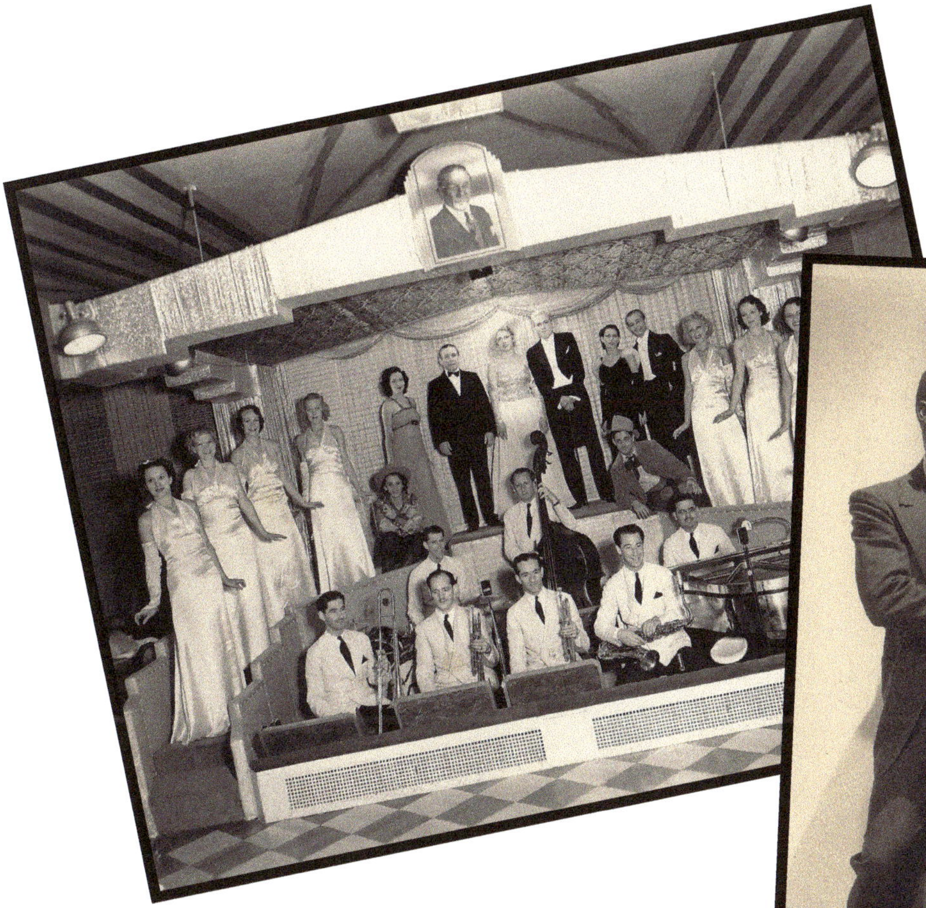

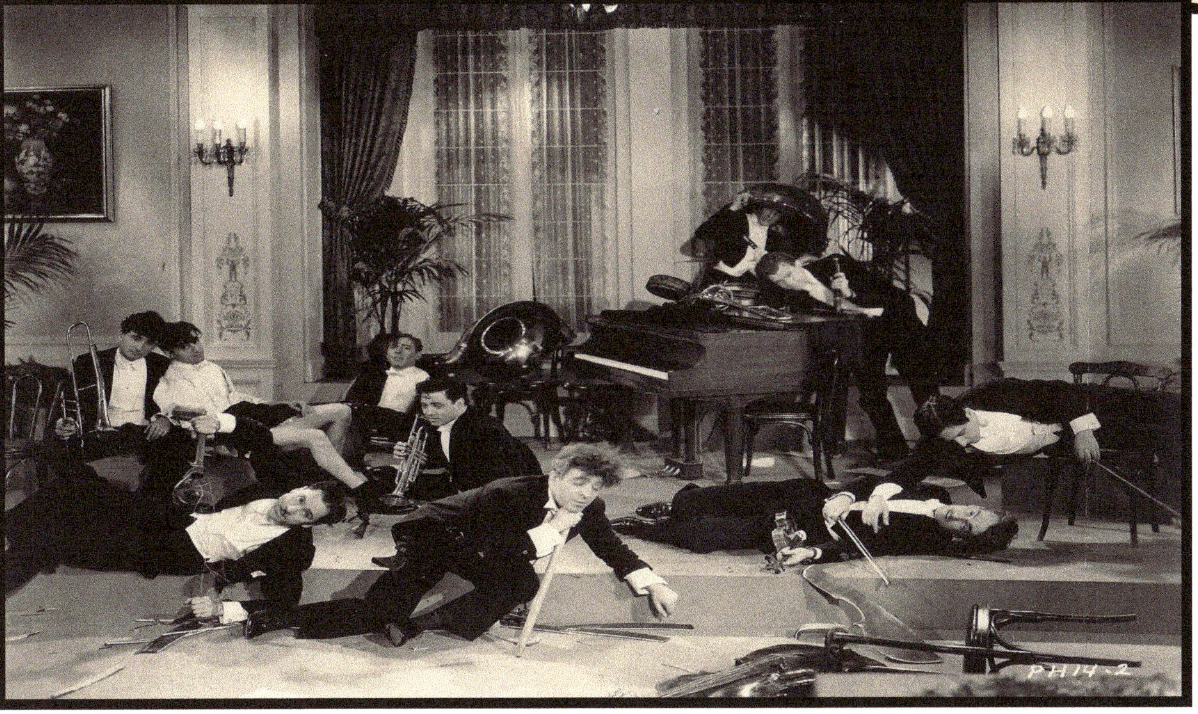

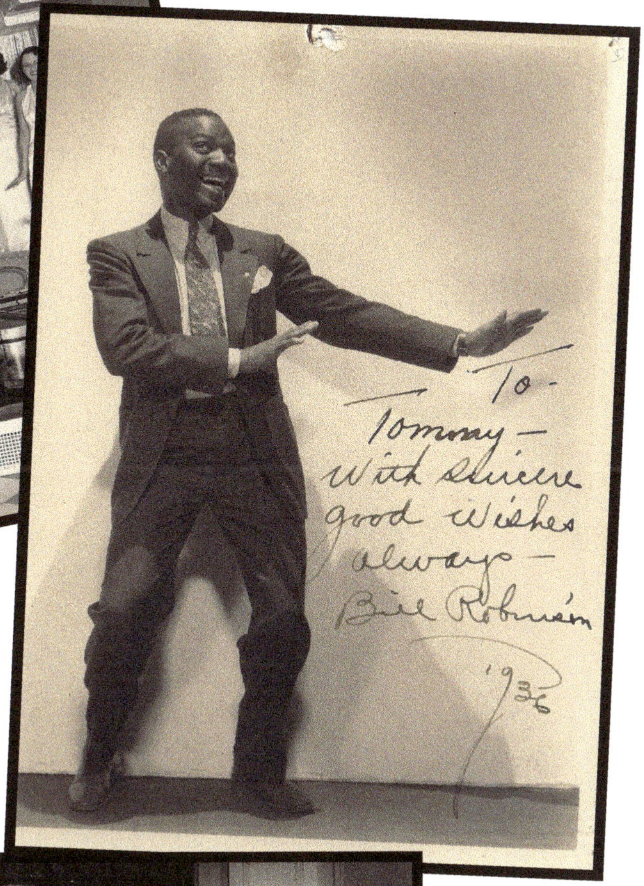
To
Tommy—
With sincere
good wishes
always—
Bill Robinson
1936

PH14-2

To Tommy Jones.
Best Wishes
Ethel Waters

PUSH
HELP
KEEP YOUR
EXPOSITION
CLEAN
POLY
16
LINCOLN
12

the basement of our 46th Ave. home. Carefully protecting these treasures we would start over in a land far away from the fog. A place without a neighborhood store or merchants that knew us by name. A place where a car would be needed to take you wherever you wanted to go.

My father stopped drinking when he found a red haired women that lived in a small apartment on Polk Street. Her name was Helen. It's hard for a child to understand the hidden currents of life but you are aware of pain and joy. A mother in grief and struggling to keep everyone together. The arrangements that are made. T.C. living two lives. Once again happy to be taking Greyhound Bus Tours with Helen. Stopping in every small town and city to play his trombone for Greyhound travelers and grab a bus station sandwich. My mother's insistence that everyone be together for family dinners and holiday celebrations.

The family gatherings and eventual love for each other simply got bigger as Helen joined us. Deanna and I got married and my mother became a dotting grandmother for our daughter Hilary. Actually, Hilary and my mother are quite alike. Stoic and stubborn without prejudice or malice in their eyes. Glenna and her two children Sandy and Jean along with my brother Doug brought spouses and their children to my mother's events. And there were always strangers welcomed to our table. Someone in need of a place to stay or a place to call home.

Christmas Eve was the one event no one was allowed to miss. It was my mother's way of bringing everyone together. I think that's what she wanted more than anything in life. To be surrounded by family. All of us. Family, co-workers, friends and anyone without a place to go for the holiday. For Glenna and my mom the preparation for this event started around Labor Day. They began to make presents in secret. Crochet projects. Sweaters to knit. Things to purchase on lay-a-way and hide throughout the house.

By early December the house was transformed into a Winter Wonderland. A one of a kind Douglas fir Christmas tree dominated the living room with its grace and fresh pine smell. It usually had more than one top to accommodate more than one angel. And it was always the first tree in the neighborhood. Lights were strung and traditional ornaments hung along with strands of ironed tinsel. Happy Holly and an assortment of plastic holiday figures poked their way between ice cycle branches and hand made decorations. Each memento had its special reserved place in the tree.

The living room was festooned with an array of tiny reindeer, colorful candles, and a miniature snow caped village. Santa's elf's and our childhood photos with the Emporium Santa Claus covered every table along with the trinkets and holiday messages that couldn't find a place on the tree. The windows were spray painted with a flocking substance that resembled snow and mistletoe dangled from the ceiling prompting unexpected hugs and lots of blushing. There was always an artificial wreath on the front door and above the fireplace mantel. The mantel was crowded with colorful Christmas Cards mailed and exchanged with friends close by and far away. Below the Christmas cards were stockings with embroidered names. Each stocking different in shape and size and hung with care in hopes T.C. would get home as fast as possible.

The preparation for this special event had nothing to do with baby Jesus. It started and became a family tradition, to accomodate T.C playing at Sweets Ballroom in Oakland and not getting home until late on Christmas Eve. His arrival signaled the beginning of our celebration. My mother could hardly contain herself. This expectation danced in her eyes and a smile that never ended. She delayed the gift giving as long as she could or we would allow. There was

Mom, T.C. and Helen

Mom, Glenna and Hilary

the buffet served on green Depression glass dishes, that only made an appearance on this special evening. Cold cuts, cheese, Pillsbury buttermilk biscuits and her piece de resistance – a red and green jello with marshmallows and pineapple filling. 'Sees' candy was displayed in the shape of Santa's sleigh and guarded by glass figurines that T.C. inevitable mistook for his, "this is the best chocolate ever".

Black vinyl 78's fell onto the Motorola turntable to fill the house with singing Chipmunks, Bing Crosby, and Etta James. Moms attempt to capture the event in 8mm film and flash bulb smiles accompanied the nervous anticipation of gifts that defied frantic shaking and speculation. A mountain of gifts were piled under the Christmas tree and spilled into the living room. Not one or two gifts from Mom and Glenna but as many as they could conjure up from mid season. All carefully and uniquely wrapped to fit the personality of each recipient. Some covered in newsprint with hand drawings. Others with notes directing the recipient to a gift in the garage or bow covered mystery in the back bedroom. And of course those envelope gifts of money hidden next to Happy Holly.

The giving of gifts was orchestrated by my mother. She appointed the youngest in the family to be Santa Claus. Then directed Santa as to which gift to past out and to whom. It allowed everyone to enjoy the excitement of a new Timex, fuzzy robe, Chia Pet, or letter to be read out loud. After a wrapping paper war, it was always a surprise to find my mother as the only one that didn't open her gifts. She had to be last. To savor every moment. It took us awhile as a family to realize what she wanted most. Something personal. A note or signed photograph. A hand crafted school project.

On one occasion we gave Mom, Glenna and T.C. something that became an integral part of every Christmas Eve. Lots of family worked on this. It was to be a surprise. Something special. Not a coat or potted plant. Not a book or tickets to a show. Not a pizza. Not a puppy or a trip or even a game. We found our perfect gift at Goodwill. A store of recycled items. Things no longer wanted. Our discovery was in a crate of lost and found shoes. Shoes with their tongues out pleading for another life. We carefully selected a pair of oversized boots, wing tips size 16, and leather slippers.

In stealth fashion we decorated each pair of shoes. The boots became complete with American flags, flying eagles, and clanking cymbals on each toe. Perfect for T.C. and his life leading a march up Grant Ave or tapping out rhythm at Sweets.

For Glenna we decorated her slippers suitable for the lead in Swan Lake. A hundred white feathers and pink ribbons that fluttered with slightest wiggle. For Mom we glow painted her giant wing tips and sprinkled it with golden sequins, glued taps to the toes and heels. Perfect for a hoofer with big feet.

Those shoes became a regular part of Christmas Eve. They found a revered place sticking out under the Christmas tree and reminding us of the love that found its way into our hearts. Laughing and sharing the greatest gift of all. Being together.

Looking back on these Christmas Eve celebrations I realize they were like the vaudeville escapades from the Fox, Orpheum and Warfield Theaters on Market Street. In preparations for the finale of gift giving there were spontaneous talent shows by all in attendance. Family stories told and retold. The same jokes about the jello or being a favored child. Photos and film from past holidays eagerly awaited as a must see. With everyone wearing hats, glasses, and waving fake cigars the children were given a box of costumes and music to dance their version of Jingle Bells or the Readers Digest interpretation of the Nutcracker. Everyone was involved in terrible attempts to sing Christmas Carols. It was the show that mattered and we were stars. And always a curtain above us, waiting to close.

For years Glenna and my mother worked for Western Union in Teletype. Standing all day feeding tape into large machines. They both died in their sleep and upon my mother's request, their ashes were carefully placed on a sunny Ben Lomond knoll under redwood trees looking out onto the Pacific Ocean. T.C. passed away in a nursing home across the street from Mt. Zion Hospital.

Mom and Glenna, best friends forever.

The greatest gift I gave to my father was in his faltering years in the nursing home. I arranged for a dance band to come play the big band scores from T.C.'s days in the band at Sweets Ballroom. He tapped his finger against the bed rail and smiled, "This is the best day ever". In this all white world Helen had scotch taped photos of T.C. playing at Sweets.

I was talking to my father not even sure if he could hear me. It was one of our regular one-way conversations. "Remember when you came to Lincoln High School to talk to the principal. The principal, Dr. Hill, wouldn't let me run for student government unless I could explain the many days I wasn't in class. And you, you told the principal I was working for you, it was an excused absence ...you, you lied to Dr. Hill, telling him I was working for you fixing up Ronnie's Doug Out #2. Dad, you lied right there in front of me!" My father T.C. Jones just looked up at me and smiled. Then T.C. passed away holding my hand. Sometimes fathers and sons don't talk a lot. Sometimes they don't have too.

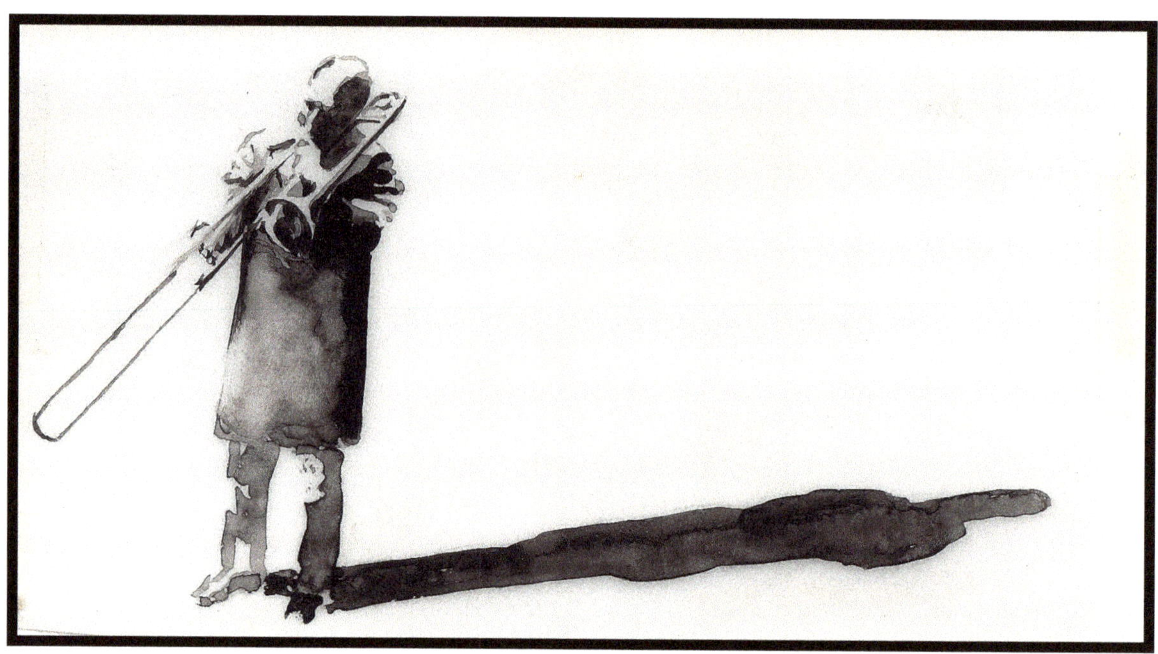

SOCIAL
Sweets
DANCING
Sweets
NORRIE PAULSEN
and HIS BAND
THUR FRI SAT SUN

10
1952
Tommy

The Chair

My father gave me one late gift in life. For 30 years T.C.'s day job was a salesman at Sterling Furniture on Market street. It was the premier furniture store on Market street located down the street from the Emporium and across from Woolworths. As a child I visited my father and watched him sell T.V.'s on the 6th floor of Sterling. These were the days before Good Guy's and a wall of 'take me' blinking T.V.'s. My father dressed in his best double breasted suit and polished shoes invited customers into a furnished room graced by a single exquisite T.V.—RCA, Zenith, or Motorola. This T.V. was a piece of furniture to accentuate any living room. My father was a good salesman. With that Irish glint in his eye and giant steps that spoke about going someplace, he could sell anything. After each sale my father pointed to heaven or as I later found out the mezzanine of the store. This was the executive suite surrounded in glass and overlooking the stores entrance and first floor.

The management of Sterling must have loved my father. They'd always have him sit in a large leather chair in the executive office and ask T.C. to work on the weekend or for a 'moonlight sale'. My father would gladly work the extra hours. "Ronnie, someday, they're going to invite me to play my horn to announce some sale or something', you'll see, they like me here at Sterling."

By the time I was in high school my father was no longer on the 6th floor selling the high commission T.V.'s but on the 4th floor selling refrigerators. I noticed his shoes were not always polished and his gait that once bounced across a room was slowed. Still, he reported how Sterling needed him. The executive team of Sterling's had my father take a seat in the large leather chair. They asked my father to talk to the men about not joining a union at Sterling Furniture. They argued that Sterling's was a family and took care of its own. "Tommy, the commissions are good, and we don't need a union with the prospect of opening a new store, and the boy's like you, talk to them, won't you Tommy." And my father would talk to the men and there would be no union at Sterling Furniture.

By the time I was living on Stanyan street with a family of my own, my father was working in the basement of Sterling selling bric brac and household wares. It was on Christmas Eve when Sterling Furniture invited my father to come and sit in the customary leather chair in the glass mezzanine. The other salespeople gathered on the first floor to look up at T.C. sitting in that familiar chair. He had been at Sterling for 30 years. There were rumors about the store moving to the new mall in Stonestown or Westlake. They knew that Tommy would be the first one to know about the move and pass on the news. As for T.C. he thought the store might finally want him to play his horn. Maybe to greet customers for the post Holiday Sales. There was always that smile on T.C.'s face as if he knew something or heard something important and joyous that evaded everyone else. I can see him sitting in that chair tapping his foot to some unheard melody. Or his favorite song 'Tea for Two'.

On that fateful Christmas Eve Sterling Furniture informed my father that this would be his last day of work at Sterling. They were cutting back and the younger men were being transferred to the new suburban store. He wouldn't be going with them.

There was no golden parachute or retirement benefit, just one more day to work! The management of Sterling thanked my father for all his years of service, then asked if they could do anything for T.C. on this last day of work. My father asked for only one thing—the chair. Sterling Furniture sold my father that chair!

Following a full day of work and checking out sales my father took the chair from its mezzanine perch. He carried that chair on his back up Market street and over the 17th street hill to my house on Stanyan street. When he put the chair down in my living room it sounded like thunder. Now fathers and sons don't talk that much, at least my dad and I never spoke about feelings or important things. But on this day we spoke a lot about what matters in life. He talked a lot about how many times he'd sat in that 'God damn chair'. How many times he didn't speak up or question what was asked of him. Pointing at the chair he made me promise, "Ronnie, don't sit down in life!"

The chair sits in my living room, It's a reminder of my father's wish. No one is allowed to sit in that large leather chair. No one!

<u>PLACE</u>

Today I carry with me the memories and lessons of my youth. To never let anyone stand at the end of a line and be denied access to the group or nation we belong to. To enrich one's life by taking in those in need. To expect the unexpected. To know there is always someone faster and bigger. To welcome into your life someone that is different. To seek out and find the love in everyone around you. To take risks and not be afraid of the unknown. To forgive those that spit on you. To find a little kindness and mint jam in everything you do. To enjoy each day and then the sunset that awaits you.

Deanna and I have shared a life together. Most of it in or around the Sunset. Our first apartment was across the street from the Surf Theater. Then a home up the street from Kezar or if you're a realtor a home in the Upper Haight or Cole Valley. We've lived and brought up our daughter Hilary in this home at 1201 Stanyan Street. Of course we took in two of Hilary's wayward friends and then we were blessed with two grandchildren - Breanna and Taylor. A life of firsts that only children can bring into a home. Meals that become traditions, science projects on the kitchen table, first day at school, parties and games under a blanket tent and one more story before we say goodnight.

Deanna and I both became teachers. In addition to a love for books and reading Deanna started a pottery studio with 6 others on 9th Ave. and Moraga. Our basement became a place to work on her pottery wheel and gather with friends for open studio. My teaching career had more stops than expected. It had a lot to do with freedom and social justice. I mean, who gets fired from a Psychiatric Hospital or a Palo Alto High School or Stanford University or the California Air National Guard? It was the 60's. Somewhere Bobby Ensign was smiling. To be continued...

Part 2 of this life saga in the 60's can be found in a self-published book—**<u>Airman.</u>**

Ron, Hilary, Taylor, Breanna and Deanna

I finally got a job and a place in life at the San Francisco Recreation Center for the Handicapped. Of course, it was located in the Sunset. The evangelical director, Janet Pomeroy, thought I'd been sent by God. Maybe it was as she said a miracle. I worked at RCH, now the Janet Pomeroy Center, for 30 years. Participated in Theatre Unlimited to tell the stories of those called disabled. Organized and coached the first San Francisco Special Olympic basketball team. A team of men and women. All ages and disabilities. We played against local teams. Pickle Family Circus, Delancey Street, The Chinese Consulate, unions, the police, and mayor's office . . . but our favorite game was against the Sisters of Perpetual Indulgence – Russian River contingent. We never lost. Of course, we cheated!!! Working at the center I was finally home. I have written about these events as a way of honoring the people that make life meaningful.

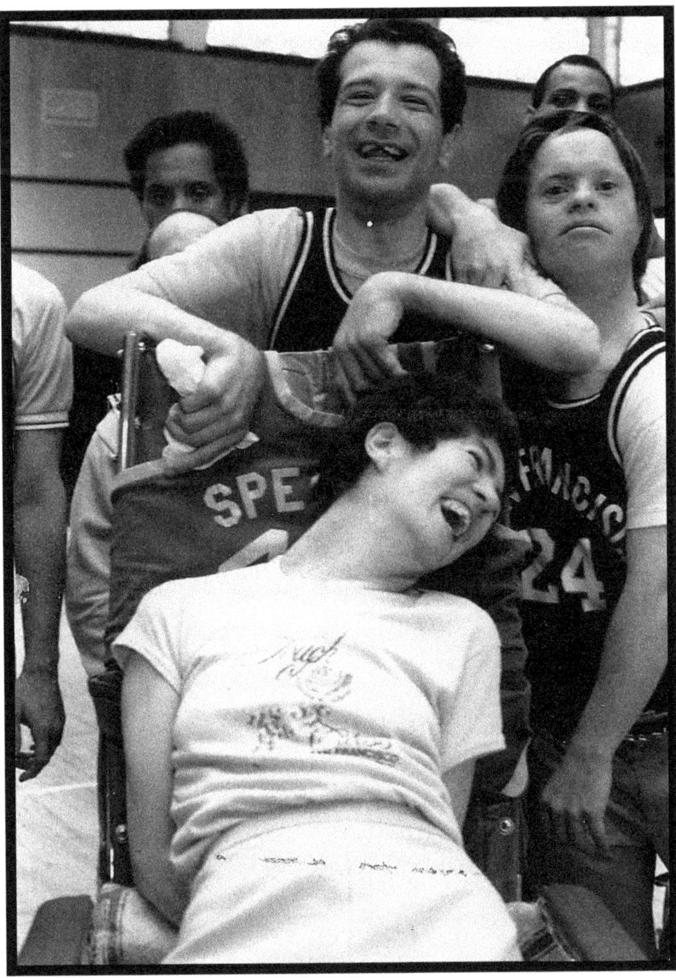

Part 3 of this life at the Center, is in a self-published book—***When God Winked***

MEMORIES

Every chance I get I drive or walk down 46th Ave. I nod or well up in tears remembering my Mom racing past me and T.C. playing his horn and declaring 'this is the best meal I've every eaten'! I think about Glenna and her two children Sandy and Jean. My brother Doug, always trying to follow me. Karl at the corner grocery store waving hello. Francisco Scott Key Annex. Bobby Ensign and his communist party. Mr. Gillman wearing those funny aviator goggles. Donald Weinstein's mother shaking my hand. A red hot Hudson and Sam Rivera from Puerto Rico. Powerhouse who would become my best friend in high school and co-conspirator drummer in our band that played Blue Moon, the one song we knew, over and over. Like my constant visits to 46th Ave. to be repeated over and over.

Sometimes there is the hint of a fire at the beach or current of fog lifting over my head and the squeal of seagulls. The familiar circle of seagulls that call me to Grandma's house. It's the one place I linger and don't ever want to leave. Grandma's house on 46th and Rivera. It's still there just as it was years ago. The miniature roses of the Insect Lady's house have mysteriously reappeared. I just stand there looking at Grandma's house. I just want to go in. See her one more time sitting at the kitchen table with Pop and Myron and Willie Acker playing Chinese checkers. Just one more time to sit at her bedside and see the full moon graced with luck.

As I stand in front of my Grandmother's house on 46th Ave. I realize I am not alone. I am simply a witness to time and place. An older Chinese couple walk past me. The man wearing a faded baseball cap. He is a step ahead of the bent over woman pulling a cart and talking into the wind. As this couple silently pass me a young woman crossed the street with a child tugging against her outstretched hand. The woman is fashionable with hipster leather boots and knitted sweater. Her child skips and reminds me of how I ran down the avenue jumping over the fingers of grass. In the beat of an eye a surfer prances toward the ocean in a wet suit and carrying a surf board. He is not wearing any shoes.

Time. And place. Passing in front of me. We are like the waves that come upon the shore full of promise only to recede. To be absorbed by the sand in glistening bubbles of light. There will be another wave behind us. Pulled by the moon and welcomed ashore. A continuum of tiny moments filled with wonder. We see each other in this moment. Passing each other in silent reverence. Another wave curling toward the sand, then vanishing in a delicate foam. All that is left is our memories.

From the beginning this place was sand and fog. Home for creatures and plants ever changing. I was there for a moment. We all have this moment, in that place we call home.

Down by the meadow
And the itty bitty pool
Swam three little fishes
And the Mommy fishy too
Swim said the Mommy fishy
Swim if you can
And they swam
And they swam
All over the dam.

<u>Acknowledgements</u>

Special thanks to the writing group at the Fromm Institute and The Marsh Theater's Club Solo for encouragement in this work. Early readers of this memoir and their helpful suggestions were provided by Doug and Marge Jones, Peggy Skaj, Christian Pease, Joanna McClure, Nina Youkelson, Mary Williams, Charlie Varon, David Ford, Gary Bacon, Malcolm Margolin, Is-e Nadel, and Cindy Spiegel. Assistance in finding and using historical photographs was provided by David Gallagher and Woody LaBounty at Western Neighborhoods Project. Initial publication of excerpts from _Life in the Sunset_ was initiated by Paul Kozakiewicz for readers of the Sunset Beacon. Transfer of photos and layout for print was facilitated by Steve Pomeroy and Mark Weisman of Regent Press. And finally, this work would not find its way to print without the love and dedication to this story by Deanna Jones.

Grandpa "Pops" on right

__Funding__

__Life in the Sunset__ is partially funded by a grant from Mel's diner in San Francisco. I guess this is what can happen when you have breakfast everyday at Mel's. You get to know the local owners Steve and Gabe along with the regulars and their stories about this city that we love. Like so many local gathering places Mel's on Geary Blvd. is scheduled to be torn down and replaced by a multple story condominium. There will be ghosts on Geary, but only a few of us will see them.

Books by Ron Jones

- *The Acorn People*
- *No Subsitute for Madness*
- *Kids Called Crazy*
- *B-Ball (The Team That Never Lost A Game)*
- *Say Ray*
- *Finding Community*
- *When God Winked and Fellini Grinned*
- *Airman*
- *Your City Has Been Kidnapped*
- *The Christmas Coat*

Reviews

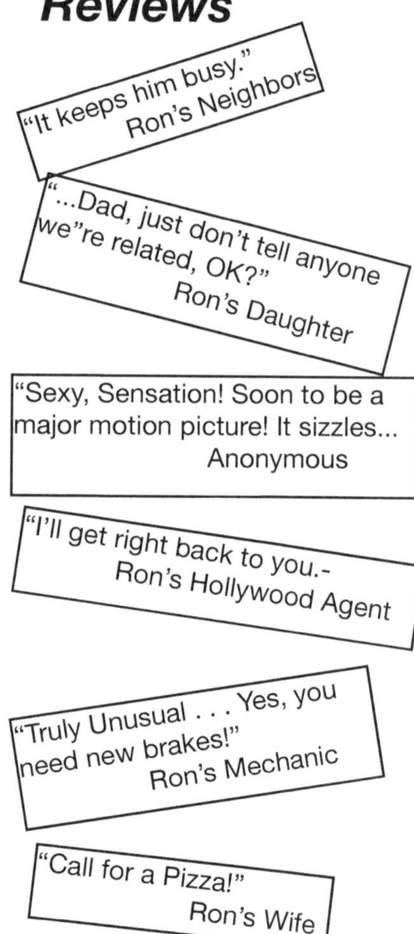

About The Author

Ron Jones is a native San Franciscan. He shares his Haight Ashbury home with his wife, daughter, grandchildren and a peaceful garden. He is a graduate of Stanford University masters degree program in education. Upon retirement from the Janet Pomeroy Center, where he taught theater and sports to the physically and mentally disabled for 30 years, he now enjoys writing and performing as a spoken word artist.

As an author he has written about everyday heroes that enrich our life. Three stories, ***The Acorn People, The Wave, and B-Ball*** have been made into television specials garnering an Emmy, Golden Globe, and Peabody for their producers. A book entitled ***Kids Called Crazy*** was nominated for a Pulitzer. And ***Say Ray*** the story of a disabled man abducted to Mexico was honored as the American Book of the Year. His classroom experiment in Fascism, ***The Wave*** has been produced as a feature film ***Die Welle*** and documentary ***Lesson Plan***. The novelized version of *The Wave,* available through Random House, is printed in 23 languages and required reading in German and Israeli schools. In 2013 Ron completed a musical version of his Wave experience. ***The Third Wave Musical*** is available through Dramatic Publishing. Theatric and musical productions of ***The Wave*** have been performed in theaters worldwide. For information, play dates, and locations see www.thewavehome.com. Ron is currently working on a play ***Kids Called Crazy*** with students at Mercy H.S. San Francisco and Marsh Youth Theater.

Recently Ron has taken the stage as a spoken word artist. Solo shows include ***Buddha Blues, Say Ray,*** and ***When God Winked***. Last year he produced his first CD, Soulful Blessing as a unique blend of poetry and jazz. For a listing of Ron's storytelling videos see www.ronjoneswriter.com.

CPSIA information can be obtained
at www.ICGtesting.com
Printed in the USA
FSHW02n2152310518
48654FS